LIGHTNING
IN A BOTTLE

> THE PROVEN SYSTEM TO
> CREATE NEW IDEAS AND
> PRODUCTS THAT WORK

David Minter & Michael Reid

SOURCEBOOKS, INC.®
NAPERVILLE, ILLINOIS

Published by Sourcebooks, Inc.
P.O. Box 4410, Naperville, Illinois 60567-4410
(630) 961-3900
Fax: (630) 961-2168
www.sourcebooks.com

Library of Congress Cataloging-in-Publication Data

Minter, David D.
  Lightning in a bottle : the proven system to create new ideas and products that work / David D. Minter, Michael Reid.
     p. cm.
  Includes index.
  ISBN-13: 978-1-4022-0734-1
  ISBN-10: 1-4022-0734-4
  1. New products. 2. Brainstorming. I. Reid, Michael (Michael James)
II. Title.

HF5415.153.M56 2006
658.5'75--dc22

                                                  2006024096

Printed and bound in the United States of America.
BVG 10 9 8 7 6 5 4 3 2 1

For Chris & Jeffrey, Suzy, my mother, and the
memory of my father.
D.D.M.

For Annie, Sam, Joe, Max, Jack, Rosa, and Beanie.
M.J.R.

ACKNOWLEDGMENTS

For all who offered their time, thoughts, and support, especially:

- Ron Castell for his generous assistance in reviewing the material on Blockbuster Video.
- H. Wayne Huizenga and George Dean Johnson Jr. for endorsing our process for developing new products.
- Allen Klose for his help and suggestions.
- Scott Beck for his suggestions on key chapters.
- Mitchell Malvan for his encouragement and suggestions.
- Mark Goldston for his suggestions on key chapters.

CONTENTS

PREFACE

Lightning in a Bottle is about ideas, and the power of ideas to transform. It is about harnessing ideas, and using the energy from ideas to achieve success beyond imagination. *Lightning in a Bottle* is about capturing pure energy.

Great thinkers throughout the ages have spoken of ideas. Ancient philosophers and presidents, businessmen and writers found eloquent ways to express the importance of ideas:

*"There is one thing stronger than all the armies in the world, and that is an **idea** whose time has come."*

—Victor Hugo, French Poet, Dramatist, Novelist

*"Everything begins with an **idea**."*

—Earl Nightingale, Radio Announcer, Author, Speaker

*"All achievements, all earned riches, have their beginning in an **idea**."*

—Napoleon Hill, Speaker, Motivational Writer

"Ideas control the world."
—James A. Garfield, Twentieth President of the United States

"If you pray for anything, let it be for an idea."
—Percy Sutton, Businessman, President of *Inner City Broadcasting*

"Eureka! I've got it."
—Archimedes, Greek Mathematician

We've been fortunate to work with folks that thought in big-whopper, stretch-your-brain-beyond-belief kinds of ways. People that have captured lightning in a bottle not once, not twice…but over and over and over again.

Here's an example. We are working for an organization in the early nineties that assembles, from scratch, one of the largest music retailers in the country. And then opens up a chain of outdoor amphitheaters around the country to put on live concerts. Before you can say rock and roll, our company has signed on to sponsor Paul McCartney's U.S. tour, and we're amazed to find ourselves sitting ten feet from Sir Paul as he announces our partnership at a press conference.

Our work in the entertainment arena, working with idea giants, brought us to enjoy many other wonderful "Eureka" moments, like…

- Cheering the Florida Marlins as they played their inaugural game as the newest member of National League Baseball (our employer's founder launched the team);
- Watching our friends and spouses dance the "twist" live onstage with Chubby Checker (brought in to entertain a group of our business partners);

- Giggling as comedian Dana Carvey makes a surprise appearance at a meeting, being announced as our new boss—and then treated to a monologue about how he plans to shake things up;
- Sitting "on the glass," watching the Florida Panthers play hockey (another professional sports team launched by the founder of a company we worked for).

Throughout this book, we often use our entertainment experiences to talk about ideas. But having worked in other industries over the years, it is crystal clear that lightning in a bottle—great, powerful ideas—create a "rush" no matter what the industry. People seem to have a sixth sense when they are working on powerful ideas—and they amass the strength to make things happen that just boggles the mind.

CHAPTER 1

LIGHTNING IN A BOTTLE

> This book is about creating
> and developing ideas that will
> drive your business.

Ideas that drive a business are the "lightning in a bottle." It is exciting to be part of the process that comes up with new ideas for products and services, and to execute them successfully. It is thrilling to make an impact with an idea you created. It is the most fun part of business. Nothing else compares.

This book talks about three kinds of ideas that are the heart of business growth:
- Ideas for new products
- New services
- Ideas for new marketing programs

These three fuel American business. Without them, business stagnates and eventually dies.

There is nothing as powerful as an idea whose time has come. Consider Blockbuster Video. The advent of the VCR in the early eighties gave birth to a new way of watching movies at home. American households couldn't rent movies fast enough. And Blockbuster couldn't open up stores fast enough—even at the torrid pace of a new store every seventeen hours. When you've got an idea that's working, it is electrifying.

Creating and developing new products, services, and marketing programs is vital.

But it is often misunderstood. And, in large companies, it is almost always inefficient. The sad truth is, businesspeople often do not give much thought to developing ideas. Therefore:

Only one in ten new products succeeds!

The chapters that follow present a better way of creating and developing ideas. Companies that use the seven-step system outlined in this book will dramatically improve their chances of creating, developing, and implementing successful ideas that drive the business. They will have more successful new product launches. Their marketing programs will drive sales.

This book is for people whose heads are "on the line" to deliver results. It is for senior executives who must deliver growth and profitable revenue in order to keep their jobs. It is for entrepreneurs who seek a better process for screening ideas. And it is suitable for large organizations that *must* have big ideas to survive.

People who work in public companies know about the pressure to perform. Whether the yardstick is comparable store sales growth or quarter-to-quarter sales increases, the feeling is universal: public companies must grow, or suffer Wall Street's wrath. The pressure of performing as a public company—that is, delivering consistent, steady growth—is what motivated us to write this book.

CHAPTER 2

A BLOCKBUSTER (VIDEO) IDEA

This book is about one thing: how to develop big ideas—ideas for new products, new services, and new marketing programs that will drive your business. Big ideas are "lightning in a bottle." It is exciting when you have one. It is exciting to be part of the thrill ride when you have crafted something that takes off with incredible velocity.

This chapter describes what it was like to be part of the thrill ride known as Blockbuster Video—back near the beginning when it was just starting. It is a story about sheer grit and entrepreneurial guts. As much as anything, the story of Blockbuster Video is about the power of a single idea to launch not just a business, but a whole new $20 billion category known as home video that did not exist before. It illustrates what can be achieved by aggregating a mass of consumers around a simple yet powerful idea.

THE BLOCKBUSTER STORY

The year is 1985, and Blockbuster store #1, at Skillman and Northwest Highway in Dallas, Texas, is about to open its doors. At the time, only a quarter of U.S. households had

VCRs. Early adopters—the folks that are first on their block to buy new electronic toys—paid $1,000 or more for a simple VCR machine, which was the size of a medium suitcase. Sony's proprietary Betamax format was in the market, in a life or death battle with the VCR format. The VCR format ultimately won, despite the fact that Betamax cassettes were smaller and produced better quality images and sound.

Pre-1985, the adventurous consumers who bought the suitcase-sized VCRs used them quite differently than today. Mostly, it was about "time-shifting"—recording a show or movie off television in order to watch later. The folks that came together to form Blockbuster Video had a very different idea about how consumers would use VCRs.

Blockbuster's vision was simple. Let consumers rent pre-recorded movies, take them home, and pop them into their VCRs. Gather the family, make some popcorn, and *viola*—a movie of your choice to watch in the comfort of your home, with no commercials. All this for a couple of dollars.

Consumers sparked to the idea of controlling their television viewing—and the rest is history.

It was all about control. Consumers loved being able to control "when" they watched and "how" they watched with the ability to pause and rewind to watch favorite scenes over and over. The VCR put consumers in control—and changed the entertainment landscape forever.

It turns out that "time-shifting," which was the original purpose for VCRs, was only the appetizer for what would come later. At the industry's peak in 2002, American consumers rented 3.5

billion movies. The average household rented thirty-four movies over the course of the year, which works out to more than a movie every other week, for every household in the country.

Consumers spend far more to rent and purchase movies than they do going to the theater, and have done so for many years. The enabling technology was the VCR. But it was Blockbuster that rolled the idea of renting movies—this lightning in a bottle—into neighborhoods across America.

How did they do this? Well, before the first Blockbuster store opened, the video rental industry was quite different from what it is today.

THE EARLY INDUSTRY

- Small stores
- Limited selection
- No videotapes on display—all were kept under lock and key in the backroom
- Expensive VCRs—$600 to $800 in the late eighties. Many first experienced this new technology by renting VCR machines for the weekend, at $20 a shot.
- Video store membership fee's of $100 to $150 per year
- Stores located in strip-mall locations—small stores and hard-to-find parking
- Poorly lit stores, especially late at night when adjoining strip-mall businesses had closed for the day
- X-Rated movies, often kept in a separate room with nothing more than a curtain and an "adults only" sign separating XXX-rated from the rest of the store

Before Blockbuster, you really had to want to rent a movie, because it was, too often, a very strange experience. The tiny video rental industry at the time was almost entirely "mom and pop" stores. You never knew quite what to expect when you walked into one of these places. Adult movies were an important ingredient in these early days of the video rental industry, and many stores were not places to take the kids. Erotic movie posters were often used to decorate the store walls.

David Cook, an accomplished entrepreneur, had become interested in the idea of opening a video store—Blockbuster Video. H. Wayne Huizenga's biography talks about the early days and the day David Cook opened the very first Blockbuster Video store.

While Blockbuster was built around a very simple idea— renting movies—opening the first store was anything but simple. David Cook spent a lot of money developing the necessary computer systems. Building and opening the first store in Dallas was hard. But the doors opened in October 1985, and consumers mobbed the place. Never before could ordinary folks get movies to take home and watch on their own schedule.

Just how different was Blockbuster when it opened its doors? Different enough to be considered "lightning in a bottle." Consider what Blockbuster Video brought to the party.

In the late eighties, Blockbuster truly had captured "lightning in a bottle."

THE BLOCKBUSTER WAY

- No X-rated tapes
- Huge selection of eight thousand movies, five to ten times as many movies as competitors at the time
- Movies out on display to look at—not hidden in a back room
- Bright, cheerful stores—bright yellow and blue
- No membership fee
- Kids play area, where small children could have fun while parents shopped for a movie
- Longer hours
- Clean, neat employees dressed in khaki pants and pale blue shirts
- Exterior lighting that made it feel safe to visit at night

Fast-forward to 2006. Blockbuster, Inc. is a NYSE listed company and is the world's leading renter of videos, DVDs, and video games with more than nine thousand stores and over seventy-three thousand employees throughout the Americas, Europe, Asia, and Australia. The company commands a 30 percent plus market share of the domestic video rental industry, and revenues exceed $5 billion a year. Two-thirds of the population in the U.S. live within a ten-minute drive of a Blockbuster store.

The VCR, in no small part due to Blockbuster, became the fastest adopted consumer technology in history and today 98 percent of American households own at least one

VCR. The only technology since to capture the consumer attention faster is the DVD player—arguably just a better way of delivering many of the same benefits the VCR ushered in.

The VCR was an unexpected boon for Hollywood. The home-video industry was an entirely new revenue stream and, in a relatively short period of time, home-video revenue became a larger revenue stream than the theatrical movie business. Amazingly, watching movies at home created more money for Hollywood than revenue acquired by folks going to theaters.

Suddenly, Hollywood studios had hope for movies that flopped at the box office. Indeed, the common business model today is for movie studios to try to at least break even during the theatrical run, and count on making money by renting and selling movies.

BEING PART OF A LIGHTNING STRIKE— BLOCKBUSTER'S FAST GROWTH

By the time we joined Blockbuster in 1991, the company had a head of steam, and about a thousand stores open. During our five-year stint as the first head of research and database marketing, Blockbuster opened a store every seventeen hours, seven days a week, 365 days a year. It was incredible to watch, and to be part of. It was a thrill ride, complete with the big scares that go along with being thrilled.

Blockbuster Video in the early days was magic—the magic of starting a fast-growing business—and the adrenaline rush of pulling it off. Lawrence Miller, author of *Barbarians to Bureaucrats: Corporate Life Cycle Strategies,* talks about how it takes a "barbarian" mentality to launch a business.

Barbarians are entrepreneurs at the core, and are most at home when they are launching new businesses.

> *No one can possibly achieve any real and lasting success or "get rich" in business by being a conformist.*
>
> —J. Paul Getty

David Cook, H. Wayne Huizenga, Steven Berrard, George Dean Johnson Jr., and Scott Beck were Blockbuster Video's prophets and barbarians. These entrepreneurs were as different as night and day, but they shared a vision and were able to see the future, which was a Blockbuster Video store in every neighborhood in America—and quickly. They saw a little "consumer-unfriendly" industry in 1985, visualized the possibilities, and then made it happen.

Prophets and barbarians rarely change coats—growth is ingrained in their DNA. Huizenga went on to form AutoNation, and is credited as the only person in U.S. business history to start three *Fortune* companies from scratch. Berrard recently formed a public company and acquired national smoothie-beverage chain Jamba Juice. His plan is to grow the business. Johnson went on to develop a revolutionary chain of extended-stay hotels—called Extended Stay America. Beck opened a chain of retail general merchandise stores in Mexico. The list of accomplishments by these folks speaks volumes about serial entrepreneurship, which is the stuff that business prophets are made of.

Barbarians don't overburden themselves with org charts, job descriptions, or complicated processes. They do not finesse their way past obstacles; they simply work hard to overcome anything and everything that stands in their way.

Prophets are the other kind of person Miller talks about that are around in the early stages of corporations. Prophets are idea people, the visionaries.

Capturing lightning in a bottle requires great ideas and great execution.
Prophets bring the seeds of ideas.
Barbarians execute those ideas.

What does this have to do with ideas and growth?

As companies become large and successful, prophets are tossed out. So are the barbarians. Which leaves the situation that big businesses face today, where one in ten ideas succeed. Why? Because the prophets—the source and energy and momentum to move new ideas forward—are gone.

Power shifts to "bureaucrats" who are great at maintaining businesses but lack the unique "big idea" skills of the prophets.

As companies get really big, someone else takes control. In the largest corporations, lawyers and professional administrators have a much larger role in running the company—because big companies have much to protect and much to lose. The "defense" takes control of the game. Everyone forgets that a good offense also wins games.

Large companies rightly must protect what they have built. These companies are not focused on *new* ideas, but on protecting what already exists—a defensive approach to protect the revenue streams built over the years.

> Where do the big ideas come from now?
> The answer is everywhere...and nowhere.

Big companies need ideas that appeal to the vast majority of their customers. It's common sense. Today's large corporations are incredibly fortunate to have large numbers of customers who love and buy their products. They are incredibly unfortunate because few have any barbarians or prophets left to help them develop tomorrow's products, to develop tomorrow's lightning in a bottle.

> The systematic approach outlined in this book—Idea Engineering—is a way for large companies to recapture the spirit of prophets—to develop high odds ideas to drive exceptional revenue and profit growth.

STEPPING ON THE GAS: ACCELERATING BLOCKBUSTER'S GROWTH

Back to Blockbuster, as a case study on growth and reinvention.

In the early nineties, Blockbuster was on a roll, showing and teaching consumers how to watch movies at home, whenever they wanted, with the ability to stop, start, and rewind/replay favorite scenes. And reaping the rewards. Did consumers LOVE renting movies? You bet!

Blockbuster did not wait for consumers to figure out that VCRs could be used to watch rented movies; they built stores on every corner, advertised like crazy, and taught consumers about the fun of renting movies.

There is an old adage that as businesspeople, we are not paid to wait. We are paid to make the tires burn today, tomorrow, next week, and next year. The approach outlined in this book suggests a very *proactive* approach to developing big ideas.

Can you generate lightning in a bottle on command? The answer is clearly YES!
Especially if you already have loyal customers. You just need to give them other stuff they want!

What was it about VCRs and renting movies that captivated the consumer imagination? Why has watching movies at home continued its dramatic growth for eighteen straight years? Home video is lightning in a bottle—really *one simple idea* that mixes just the right blend of four magical ingredients:

- **Choice**—thousands of movies to pick from
- **Convenience**—get a movie to watch right in the neighborhood, then return home, put on PJs, and relax
- **Control**—ability to start, stop, or pause the movie—answer the doorbell, watch half of the movie today and half tomorrow, rewatch favorite scenes
- **Value**—Renting and buying movies and video games was, and is, a great value. For four bucks, the whole family can watch a movie. Less expensive than a box of popcorn at the theater! Especially for families with kids, movies at home are far more of a value and far more convenient than loading up everyone in the car and going to a theater.

Were there mistakes in building the video giant? Of course. If you never fail, it just means you are never taking chances, and Blockbuster took plenty of them. Perhaps the most dramatic failure was an adventure into the music retailing business. Through acquisitions, Blockbuster Music quickly became the number-two music retailer in America. The winning formula for Blockbuster Video was carefully applied to Blockbuster Music. But to our shock and surprise, we got *completely opposite* results.

Regional music chains were acquired, the old store signs were ripped down, and the stores were renamed Blockbuster Music. Teams tore down all the tacky posters, beefed up the selection, put everyone in blue shirts and khaki pants, got rid of employee facial hair, tattoos, and nose rings, and started the advertising engine. When this approach was used for video stores, immediate and dramatic sales gains resulted. Not so with music; the immediate effect was that sales took a drop, and stayed there. Ouch.

Blockbuster's investment and ownership position in Discovery Zone—a children's play area with rides and slides—was another idea that never got traction. But again, the management team was smart enough to manage the investment in new ventures such that it never really hurt the core company.

Dramatic growth doesn't happen by sitting around and doing what you did yesterday—and these guys were masters at pushing ahead and trying new things. And we were all growth junkies.

One interesting twist to Discovery Zone was the invention of an adult version—called Block Party. Here is how Block Party came to be.

A curious thing happened when we talked to moms and dads about their kids and Discovery Zone; they sheepishly revealed that they would like something like it for themselves. The same thing, but "sized up" for adults.

Adults, especially young adults, like to play, and they liked the idea of crawling through tunnels and doing the kind of stuff their kids were doing at Discovery Zone. So we opened a couple of prototypes. The concept was ultimately judged not worth pursuing for a variety of reasons—several surprises along the way included having to police lewd behavior in the dimly lit tube maze.

> **Dramatic growth doesn't happen by sitting around and doing what you did yesterday—these guys were masters at pushing ahead and trying new things.**

Being "business barbarians" and entrepreneurs at heart, Huizenga, Berrard, Beck, and Johnson all went on to other ventures—some succeeded, others didn't.

Over the years, it became clear that the real "magic touch" for these men was less about magic and more about perseverance and the guts to swing the bat. Sometimes you get a home run like Blockbuster, other times you strike out or maybe get a single. But the thing that makes these four guys remarkable is that they were always in the game, always swinging (and with a batting average far better than the one in ten for most of American businesses).

> It became clear that the real "magic touch" was less about magic and more about perseverance.

Fast forward to 2006 again. Blockbuster Video faces a new challenge as the industry grows beyond renting movies to selling DVDs and renting movies online that are delivered to your door by the U.S. mail. It is a major change that will require nerves of steel, finesse, and capturing lightning in a bottle once again. Is it likely that Blockbuster can capture lightning in a bottle again? Will they make it?

Consider the fact that naysayers have been burying Blockbuster for fifteen years. Video on demand (VOD) was going to make the company a dinosaur back in 1990. And then again in the late-nineties, VOD and Internet delivery were going to sink the company. Turned out to be a bad joke on the cable companies and Telcos, as they sunk $100 billion plus into infrastructure before they learned it was not going to be that easy to steal consumers away from video stores.

Blockbuster still survives, while the cable operators and Telcos slip into reorganizations, massive write-offs, and slowdowns. Who was right?

For the future, we will just have to wait and see. The next chapter of Blockbuster will be without Viacom as a corporate parent—as this book was written, Viacom spun Blockbuster off as a totally freestanding public company again. The business of renting movies continues. But it gets tougher every day as consumers have more choices for watching movies.

Does lightning strike twice in the same spot? And if it does, can it be captured in a bottle? Your brain tells you no—but the history of this scrappy company says maybe so.

CHAPTER 3

THE PROBLEMS WITH HOW NEW PRODUCTS ARE DEVELOPED TODAY

Delivering steady, consistent growth is very difficult. One of the reasons it is hard is that there has not been a reliable process for developing new stuff. There is finally a better way to develop ideas. It's called Idea Engineering, and it works.

> Idea Engineering is not fancy theory. It's a survival program for growing profitable revenue written by people who have lived it.

The foundation for the Idea Engineering process is not complicated or mysterious. In fact, it is nothing more than the scientific process taught in third grade. The scientific process goes like this:

1. Study the subject
2. Form a hypothesis
3. Test the hypothesis
4. Adjust variables
5. Retest hypothesis

Yet the scientific process is not, in our experience, anything like the way new ideas are developed in most companies, even in companies that have structured, proactive new product approaches. The way businesses come up with ideas is more like science run amok.

Ideas for new products and services usually come in one of the following ways. These are the culprits that have led us to a shamefully low new-product success rate.

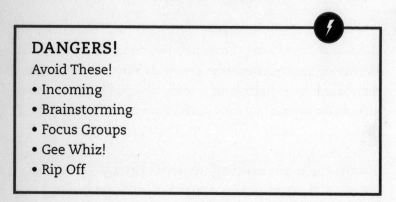

DANGERS!
Avoid These!
• Incoming
• Brainstorming
• Focus Groups
• Gee Whiz!
• Rip Off

Let's briefly examine each of these. An understanding of the tools used to develop new products will illuminate why new products so often fail when they get to the market.

Incoming

Incoming best describes where most ideas come from today. It is an unstructured system by which ideas come up through the ranks, down from the top, from the advertising and marketing people, you name it.

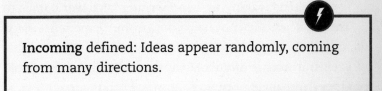

Incoming defined: Ideas appear randomly, coming from many directions.

Various people, including senior management, come up with ideas. Senior management lobs incoming ideas into the organization because there aren't enough good ideas coming from anywhere else.

Ideas that flow from the top are often implemented without proper evaluation. Why? Because until now there has not been a *reliable process* to evaluate ideas. Since we don't have a way of knowing which ideas are good, we'll do what the boss wants. That way, if it tanks, there will be less bloodshed.

Brainstorming

Here is the way brainstorming works. Bring a group of people together from different parts of a company. Create an uninhibited, free-flowing environment that will foster fresh thinking and new ideas. With brainstorming, the two basic principles are: one, come up with as many ideas as possible (assuming that quantity will produce quality), and two, defer judgment (meaning there are no bad ideas).

Creative exercises are often used to loosen up the groups thinking. Creative exercises take many forms, such as:

- Cutting pictures and words from magazines and pasting them together to make a collage
- Handing out pads of Post-It notes and writing as many ideas as fast as you can for fifteen minutes
- Listening to meditative music while lying on your back, then "waking up" and writing whatever comes to mind

Brainstorming is often a last resort, when the "idea pool" looks really, really empty.

> Brainstorming is often preceded by a feeling of desperation, because it usually means the organization is short of ideas.

Brainstorming—kind of a gold standard for idea development—is more fully explored in chapter 5. For now, let's take a quick look at what would happen if we took the business brainstorming model, and used it to solve scientific problems or to invent cures for diseases.

IF SCIENTISTS USED BUSINESS BRAINSTORMING INSTEAD OF A SCIENTIFIC PROCESS...

- Get a bunch of scientists in the lab, and hand out random containers of unlabeled chemicals and a random selection of scientific instruments.
- Have the scientists count off by threes. All the threes form a team in this corner, all the twos in

another corner, the ones in another. No regard for expertise or specialty—just random groups.

- **Instruction:** We want a LOT of mixtures, compounds, and unusual procedures. Go for quantity—there are no bad mixtures, compounds, or procedures. So try every combination of chemical and scientific process that occurs to you.

Don't worry if your mixtures don't make any sense.

Does this sound like a way to cure polio or develop the next breakthrough in interstellar space exploration? Or how Thomas Edison might have gone about inventing the light bulb? Obviously not.

Yet this is exactly how today's "idea brainstorming" sessions typically work in corporate America. The approach is lots of people, no bad ideas, go for quantity over quality, etc., etc. The problem is, it simply doesn't work.

While there are examples of how "fuzzy" scientific exploration and extremely long product development cycles can drive new product innovation (3M Corporation being a good example), most of us have more pressing new product schedules.

Doing "creativity exercises" that are supposed to loosen the brain and let the creative juices flow puts too much emphasis on innate originality and not any at all on the preliminary work necessary to come up with great ideas.

> Being creative is necessary in developing new ideas, but there has to be a *foundation* for the creativity.

What kind of preliminary work should be done?
- Learn and read everything you can *before* you jump into brainstorming and try to come up with ideas.
- Understand the problem and/or situation *before* you try to tackle solutions.
- Develop working theories that encompass what you have learned.

This preliminary work usually takes fifty to one hundred man-hours, and is best conducted by a very small team that can immerse themselves. For the same reasons scientists study their subject at the beginning, we need to do the same. Starting with creative brainstorming before doing preliminary work—the learning and working theories—is a recipe for disaster.

Don't be fooled into thinking creativity itself is the goal. Do your preparation and homework first. Strive instead for *disciplined* innovation.

Focus Groups

We hear the term focus groups all the time, but what exactly *is* a focus group?

Focus groups work like this—assemble eight strangers in a room to talk. Have a ninth stranger, called a moderator, lead the talk.

Focus groups usually last two hours, and are observed from behind a one-way mirror by a group of marketing, advertising, and other business people. Participants in the groups are asked to reveal their innermost thoughts and feelings. At the end of the two hours, another eight strangers are brought in, and the process is repeated.

In these sessions, companies listen to consumers react to their ideas. These can be ideas that have come out of the brainstorming sessions or they can come from other places.

> Focus groups are popular because they are fast, relatively inexpensive, and lull companies into believing they have learned what consumers want.

In our opinion, focus groups, while great for some things, are ineffective in developing new ideas. In fact, we believe they are a waste of time. Groups are too artificial for determining reactions to new ideas (and almost no good at all for coming up with new ideas). Consumers rarely make buying decisions in a group. Certainly, they do not make buying decisions while discussing that decision with a room full of strangers. What we've learned over the years is that market researchers believe they are getting the truth in focus groups used for exploring new product ideas, but they usually aren't. As often as not, groups provide an incorrect assessment of what consumers really want.

Focus groups are usually held in the evening, with the first group starting at 6 p.m., and the second starting at 8 p.m. and ending at 10 p.m. After that, there is usually an hour or so spent discussing what was heard by the folks in the backroom. So the marketing and other folks, after working all day, wrap up about 11 p.m. Fifteen-hour days are the rule when working with focus groups.

Often, focus groups are held in two or three different cities, on back-to-back days. Visiting multiple cites is based on the theory that consumers in different cities will say different things. So the marketing folks that are running the show have to travel from city to city during the day to be ready for nighttime groups. It's grinding work—long hours and travel.

> **None of this leaves much time for thinking about what you are hearing—you are on the run, rushing through the whole thing.**

Focus groups are good for some purposes—but they are a poor way to develop new products and services.

Gee Whiz!

With so many new products and services being driven by technology, there is a need for "raw innovation." By raw innovation, we mean technology-based building blocks that are the springboard for new products. An example of raw innovation is the integrated circuit. Born out of the U.S. space program, one integrated circuit can replace millions of transistors and other electrical components. Integrated circuits spawned thousands of new consumer products that simply would not have been possible without this raw innovation; cell phones, personal computers, and DVD players, to name just a few. Large companies invest a lot of time and money to come up with new technologies like the integrated circuit. Raw innovation is a great hallmark of American business; this willingness to invest in technology has changed the world. "Gee Whiz!" is not the same thing as raw innovation.

Here's what we mean by Gee Whiz! and how it creates problems. Too often, new products move from research labs to market without finding out if anyone wants to buy them. It works like this: R&D came up with it. It is really neat. Sometimes consumers agree and the gizmo is a hit. Sadly, that is usually not the case.

Very often, if R&D has not involved the consumer in the development of the gizmo, the public does not care. You have a product "in search of a market." But it doesn't sell. And then heads roll.

The trick is to apply raw innovation to products that will sell. Up until now, there has not been a good "early on" process for taking these amazing Gee Whiz! innovations and determining true consumer interest. For now the focus is on how *not* to develop products. Later, there will be a clear and simple solution—a process to follow to know what products will sell and what products will not sell.

Rip Off

"Rip off" is just like it sounds. Just wait for competitors to come up with something—then copy it. This is actually the best approach of all the ones we listed. Stealing a proven idea will result in a much better percentage of hits than pet projects, brainstorming, focus groups, or R&D running amok. The reason is that the competition has already been through twenty failures before you see the one success in the marketplace (the surviving ideas in the market are the winners).

For some companies, the strategy is to invest nothing in new product development. Rather, they let competitors spend their time and money. When the competitor comes up with an idea that works, they steal it.

Rip off as a source of ideas is cost effective. But companies whose new idea strategy is built around theft end up a "me too," not market leaders. They are almost always in the back of the pack.

There are a lot of ways to go wrong when developing new products. It could be focus groups, where you think you learned what consumers want but often haven't; or Gee Whiz! when an engineering team creates a "product in search of a market," where demand may be nonexistent. Or you may rip off a competitor, which can work, but is rarely the stuff of perennial winners in the business world. None of these will take you to the next level, where successful products are the norm and new product failures are the exception.

NEW IDEAS—NETTING IT DOWN

The new-idea creation and development process in American business is broken. Instead of using a solid, proven process that yields successful new products that consumers want to buy, businesspeople too often spin their wheels. Trying to use tools like those discussed previously just doesn't work. It's not because of lack of initiative—plenty of time and effort are poured into new product development. The problem, up until now, has been the lack of a proven process for developing new products. The pain from using today's broken process has not escaped witty observation. A new product director presented the following flow chart to show how the idea process was supposed to work in his company and how it actually worked.

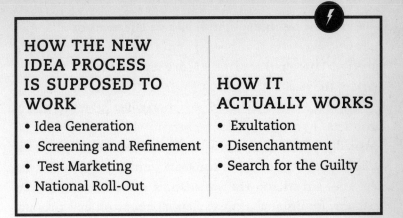

HOW THE NEW IDEA PROCESS IS SUPPOSED TO WORK	HOW IT ACTUALLY WORKS
• Idea Generation • Screening and Refinement • Test Marketing • National Roll-Out	• Exultation • Disenchantment • Search for the Guilty

Shown in Uran and Hauser's *Design and Marketing of New Products,* 1980

Why should idea development—coming up with ideas that will drive the business—be different than other business activities? There are lots of good books written on quality control, good hiring practices, and how to achieve accurate accounting reports. If there were not, if these things were left to chance, business might look like this:

- Only one in ten products manufactured would be defect-free and good enough to sell.
- Only one in ten people hired would be good hires.
- Only one in ten accounting reports would be accurate.

That is not the case. We have quality assurance systems, personnel systems, and accounting systems (post-Enron, at least). But, crazy as it is, we do not have reliable systems or processes when it comes to developing ideas that will drive the business. Only one in ten ideas succeeds—and that is somehow accepted. But business will die without new ideas.

Ideas are the last thing that should be left to chance.

> ## Nothing much has been written on how to develop winning ideas. What's needed is a "how to" recipe.

Oddly, other than books on how to brainstorm, there is little written about how to come up with ideas that drive the business. Urban and Hauser's *Design and Marketing of New Products,* for instance, an excellent textbook on new product development, spends less than 5 percent of its text on "Methods of Generating Ideas" and focuses on what to do with an idea once you have one.

So what's the solution?

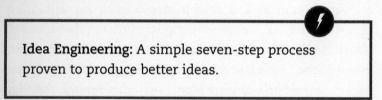

Idea Engineering: A simple seven-step process proven to produce better ideas.

Idea Engineering is a system that works better than brainstorming, focus groups, or any of the other ways ideas come to be. It is a simple-to-understand seven-step system:

1. Learn
2. Develop "Working Theories"
3. Develop ideas (concepts) from the "Working Theories"
4. Do financial Due Diligence

5. Talk to consumers—not in focus groups, but one at a time
6. Iterate the concepts by listening to consumers
7. Take the best concepts coming out of the interviews and "monetize" them—predict their real world revenue

Each of these steps is illustrated using case studies in the following chapters.

Beyond describing the seven steps and how to use them, we include chapters that will help you avoid common idea-development pitfalls. Many of the principles in this book are very different than what you have read in marketing and business literature. The tools and processes for developing new products are deeply engrained in the business world. There is a certain amount of unlearning that needs to be embraced in order to move beyond the current mediocre success rates for new products. The next several chapters provide a primer on how new products are developed today—along with the pitfalls and problems inherent in today's broken process. It is important to understand how *not* to develop new products; doing so is the first step in the journey to learning a better way. The better way—Idea Engineering—will be presented later in a simple how-to fashion that will transform how you develop new products.

CHAPTER 4

THE UPSIDE-DOWN PYRAMID— OR HOW IDEAS ARE DEVELOPED IN CORPORATE AMERICA

This chapter presents a series of short case studies on new products. The accounts are firsthand descriptions of how well-meant new product efforts went awry. The companies behind the stories are all household names. The point is that no corner of American business is void of bad practices when it comes to new products. The problem is epidemic. It is therefore vital to understand, at a deep level, how ideas are developed today, and to understand why traditional approaches often result in failure. This is the critical first step in understanding how to do it better.

Many readers will identify with the almost comedic way new products are often developed. The stories are humorous now, but we not nearly as funny at the time, when the pressure was on to deliver winners.

Where and how does the new product ball start rolling? Oddly, businesses and businesspeople usually don't spend a lot of time thinking about new ideas. That is, until somebody realizes there are no ideas ready for market that will achieve financial success.

And then, ideas for new products and services arrive from all kinds of places in a random, disorganized fashion. Kind of like the alligator game in the arcade—heads pop up in a chaotic way.

Instead of spending the time to properly evaluate these ideas, the race is on to implement them—the next quarter will be here before you know it. Got to move, got to get them done. And the quality of the ideas—whether they will produce revenue—becomes lost in the rush. The important thing is to form the team, have the meetings, create the documents, write the training manuals, et cetera.

This is an *upside-down* pyramid—a pyramid standing on its tip. The tip of the pyramid is the idea—almost no time or effort has been put into whether this idea really has consumer appeal or whether it will produce revenue. The broadening pyramid is all the effort put into executing the idea—forming the team, getting cross-departmental support, making up important names for different parts of the execution, and on an on. All that effort on a foundation as small as the tip of an upside-down pyramid.

Here are some typical ways and case studies as to how ideas "happen" in corporate America. These are the ways ideas become upside-down pyramids.

CASE STUDY
OLD FASHIONED RIP OFF— STEALING IDEAS FROM COMPETITORS
The Case of "Most Excellent Coffee"

Stealing ideas from competitors is a common and time-honored source of new product, service, and marketing ideas. See something in the marketplace that seems to be working for a competitor? Not protected by patent or otherwise? Take it!

"Most Excellent Coffee" was a rip-off-the-competition attempt. Here we have a small, upstart restaurant chain—let's call it Jimmy's Diner—competing in the "fast casual" part of the market. Fast casual dining is do-it-yourself service (no table service) in an environment a little nicer than fast food, along with somewhat higher quality than fast food, and priced at $6 to $8 a person. Fast casual players include Chipotle Mexican Grill, Quiznos, Panda Express, and up and coming Noodles & Company.

Jimmy's Diner focuses on breakfast and lunch, and sales are okay. But the CEO of Jimmy's Diner sees Starbucks across the parking lot and Starbucks' sales are more than okay. They are fabulous (and all they are selling is coffee!). The CEO of Jimmy's Diner wants fabulous. Then his stock will rise and he can buy a place in Hawaii.

Here is the CEO's thinking—Jimmy's Diner will offer coffee like Starbucks' and siphon off some of that huge Starbucks traffic. How hard can it be to make great coffee?

The most excellent coffee team forms... Meetings are held... Sub-committees are formed... The inverse pyramid grows.

The mission: develop a better coffee program that will entice some Starbucks customers to jump ship, and come to Jimmy's Diner. After all, Jimmy's has food, and Starbucks did not at the time (except for something called scones and a few other assorted pastries).

But an analysis of Starbucks, early on, shows that much of their sales are in specialty coffee drinks—lattes, cappuccinos, and the like—selling at more than $3 a cup. Starbucks' success is not driven by plain old coffee-coffee. To make the lattes and cappuccinos and frappachinos and other specialty coffee drinks, you need a sophisticated piece of equipment, and trained operators (called baristas)—at least that is how Starbucks does it.

The idea of buying an expensive piece of equipment and having trained, skilled operators to make coffee drinks is unappealing to the Most Excellent Coffee Team at Jimmy's Diner—too much trouble, more employees, constant training.

So the team searches for alternatives. And it finds…a fully automatic cappuccino/latte/espresso maker. Plug it in, set the dial to "latte," sit back, and wait for the machine to produce the drink. The machine is expensive, but eliminates the need for those expensive baristas.

The fancy new automated machines are ordered and installed. The market test begins. A few weeks go by. And…

PROBLEMS!

Coffee sales at Jimmy's Diner pick up a bit, but not near enough to justify the expense of those fancy automated coffee machines. Suddenly, it is not going to be easy to steal Starbucks customers.

Starbucks customers like Starbucks. A lot. Among other things, Starbucks has introduced a new language to American coffee lovers, and the language is part of the Starbucks ritual—"I'd like a half-caf caramel skinny macchiato, no foam, and with an extra shot." Say what?

And Starbucks customers like the manually operated coffee machine, run by the mysterious and expert barista. Starbucks customers find that if they come a few times a week, the people behind the counter know their usual order, and start getting their drink ready as soon as they walk into the store. Jimmy's Diner, with its fancy automated specialty-coffee machine, operated by a minimum wage employee de jour, really is going to have a hard time stealing Starbucks customers.

Jimmy's Diner was taking on a very, very tough competitor. Howard Shultz, founder of Starbucks, said it in the title of his book, *Pour Your Heart Into It: How Starbucks Built a Company One Cup at a Time.*

- **Starbucks has great coffee.**
- **They DO pour their heart into it.**
- **This is as much Starbucks' magic as the coffee.**

In the end, Jimmy's Diner was not going to pour its heart into serving better coffee. Jimmy's would put a little more effort into it, but nothing more. Jimmy's had a whole kitchen to run, and all the hassle that comes along with it.

Jimmy's stole a competitor's idea that was working, but neither the CEO nor the Most Excellent Coffee Team understood the idea—specialty coffee—well enough to realize it would not work at Jimmy's. Much more time was spent on finding a latte machine than on understanding what really makes Starbucks' business tick.

The idea was the tip of an upside-down pyramid. And Jimmy's wasted a lot of time and money.

CASE STUDY
THE GEE WHIZ! FACTOR—NEW PRODUCTS DRIVEN BY INVENTION
The Weather Alert Radio Case

The Gee Whiz! factor is another way companies get ideas. Here, R&D comes up with a new gizmo. Gee Whiz! happens more often at technological and engineering-based companies, but it can strike any company. Our company in this case is well-known. It is large, and it holds thousands of patents.

Let's go back in time. It is the early 1980s. Across the United States, a vast weather monitoring and alert system is being installed. The purpose of the system: provide official U.S. Weather Service weather twenty-four hours a day via the radio. One feature of the system is an electronic alert, allowing the government to notify the public to rapidly changing and dangerous weather conditions.

Our company manufactures many things, including radios. It thinks: it would be cool to build a special purpose weather-alert radio, a stand-alone radio that only picks up the special weather channels. The radio will sit quietly until bad weather threatens, then beep and turn itself on, alerting all within hearing to the danger.

> **Name—Weather Alert Radio**
> **Cost—$300 (1980 dollars)**
> **Target—schools and other institutions that have a special need for accurate and timely weather information**
> **Part of the Pyramid: The Tip (Upside-Down)**

The company's assumption was that, well, the government built a national weather alert system, so people would pay money for a device to access to the system.

Teams were formed. Sub-committees sprouted. The pyramid grew, upside-down.

The company spent much more time working on the specifications for the radio and the manufacturing processes than it spent on the idea itself—that is, whether anyone would buy the radio or not. They never asked customers if they would buy it.

The Weather Alert Radio is built. It works great. No question, the company can build quality products (we still have one twenty years later). The warehouse is filled with Weather Alert Radios. The company says: let's get out there and sell them now!

PROBLEM!

Nobody wants to buy a weather alert radio. There is plenty of free weather information available—even in 1982. (And, by the way, this is a true story. It sounds too dumb to be true, but this kind of thing happens in American business each and every day.)

So the Weather Alert Radios stayed in the warehouse. They may still be there. And the moral of the story is: just because you can manufacture something does not mean anybody will buy it. And the other moral of the story is: don't let your company's ideas be the tip of an upside-down pyramid.

CASE STUDY
"INCOMING"—IDEAS APPEAR RANDOMLY AND TAKE ON A LIFE OF THEIR OWN

The DO-GEL (pronounced dough-gul)

"Incoming" is another way big companies get ideas. Ideas appear randomly, often from the upper levels of the organization or from outside the organization, and then take one a life of their own. Incoming can build some really spectacular pyramids.

So let's talk about the Do-gel. It is a fairly well-known company. The company sells bagels. We'll call the company The Bagel Seller. The meeting is a herd of vice presidents and an outside food consultant. The food consultant, hired by someone or another and determined to deliver a new whiz-bang idea, says, "I've got a great idea for a new product that I have been saving just for you, because you are special. It's the Do-gel. Everybody loves a donut. You marry up the sweetness of a donut with your bagels, boy oh boy, you've really got something. 'Do' from donut, plus 'gel' from bagel and we're talking Do-gel—get it? What I'm talking about is tapping into the huge donut market. The American public eats twenty donuts for every bagel it chews on."

Now this sounds like one of the dumbest ideas of all time. A flopping-fish idea—one you should just ignore until it stops flopping. Except that some folks in the room like the idea of the Do-gel. There could be something there. Could be some traction.

And the pyramid grows. Upside-down.

NOTE: Read the following from the bottom up

Consultants get involved
Weekly progress reports
Marketing messages
Weekly meetings
Sub-committees
Teams formed
Flopping-
fish
idea

PROBLEM!

Say, what is the product going to be, anyway? A low-calorie donut? But aren't donut eaters pretty happy with high fat, high sugar donuts? Even after a lot of time and effort and damaged brain cells, nobody could figure out what this thing was going to be.

Fortunately, the do-gel died quietly, before it got to market. Everybody realized the idea had no merit.

Do-gels, in the end, were an "incoming" idea that had no basis in anything other than wishful thinking that "it would be great to tap into the huge doughnut industry." Like most random, incoming ideas, it didn't fly because it had no grounding in what consumers want to buy.

CASE STUDY
HEY, LET'S DO SOME FOCUS GROUPS
We've Got a Hit!

Most everybody has heard this one. "Let's do some groups." Meaning focus groups—panels of eight to ten people selected to represent a broader population, led a by professional moderator. Focus groups are probably the most common way new ideas are screened and evaluated with consumers.

Sounds scientific, doesn't it? Sounds like this approach would produce a regular pyramid, not an upside-down one. After all, you are asking consumers if they like the idea or not.

Sadly, focus groups do not usually work when it comes to screening new concepts and ideas. They are a huge waste of time and, as often as not, produce an incorrect assessment as to what consumers want and do not want (more on why later in the book).

The company in this case study is a big recording label. You have heard of this company. Most likely you have CDs at home produced by this company.

This company has a new guy in the A&R department (the job of the A&R department is to find new talent)—let's call him Dave. Dave is twenty-four, a recently graduated MBA, and, also, the nephew of the president of the company.

After a couple of weeks on the job, Dave learns that the odds of a new artist "making it"—recording a song that will get on the charts or an album that will sell more than a few thousand copies—is terribly low. About 10 percent of the new artists the label signs make it.

Dave, business school graduate, MBA, goes to the head of the A&R department and says, "You know, we could dramatically increase our odds of signing successful new talent if we did market research." The head of the A&R department, who left school after the eighth grade, would like to say to Dave, "Punk, we're not making widgets here. This is art. You can't do market research on art."

But the head of A&R cannot say that, because Dave is the nephew of the president, so he says instead, "What did you have in mind?"

Dave says, "We're considering signing The XYZ Band, right? Before we do, let's conduct four focus groups and see if consumers will buy their record." The head of A&R says okay, only because Dave is nephew of the president.

Dave is pretty happy. He is bringing sophisticated market research methods into the antiquated music business. This could be big not just for the business, but for Dave personally. If Dave is responsible for improving the label's batting average, he could move up pretty quickly in the organization.

The XYZ Band is heavy metal, so four groups worth of heavy metal fans are recruited to come to a market research facility. The moderator sits in a conference room with the heavy metal music fans and plays them some of XYZ's music. Then he asks them if they will buy XYZ's album. Dave sits behind a one-way mirror and listens.

Group I. It is all good. They love the XYZ Band. The moderator asks how many will buy the record. There are eight heavy metal music fans in the group. Eight hands go up. Looks like we are going to sign the XYZ Band.

We've Got a Hit!

Group II. Same night. Another eight heavy metal fans. The moderator asks how many will buy the record. No hands go up. They hate XYZ Group. This does not seem right. How is it possible that **all** the people who love XYZ were in one group and **all** the people who hate XYZ were in another group?

Oh, well, there are two more focus groups the next night. We'll see what the next two say.

The next night, the same thing happens. One group loves XYZ, one group hates XYZ. Dave senses that something is wrong with the focus-group process. But how can it be wrong? They taught him the concept in business school. Maybe the moderator messed up. Maybe the people in the focus groups were not really heavy metal fans or maybe some were and some were said they were, but really weren't.

PROBLEM!

Dave cannot go back to his boss and say the market research did not work. He went out on a limb to get the research done, and he just spent $25,000 to hire a focus group moderator, recruit music fans to show up, rent a facility for conducting the groups, etc. He has to make a decision. But how can he decide? Two groups love XYZ, two groups hate XYZ. They cancel out. He is back where he started, actually worse than when he started, because he is confused as to what happened with the focus groups.

So Dave flips a coin. The coin says sign XYZ, so the label signs XYZ. XYZ's songs do not chart, and their album does not sell. Dave does not move up in the organization, even though his uncle is president. And Dave does not know what the heck happened.

Here is what happened: Dave used the wrong tool to find out what consumers want and do not want (we talk about the right tools in subsequent chapters). Focus groups do not work when it comes to new ideas (or new music artists). Dave's instinct was good—he tried to get consumer input so he would not end up with an upside-down pyramid. But he did not know the right way to do it.

CASE STUDY
BRAINSTORMING

We're Going to Make a Fortune with Bundled Broadband

Brainstorming is another way companies come up with new ideas today. Brainstorming is getting a group of people together, with the purpose of coming up with new, fresh thoughts.

> **Brainstorming has value. But it is almost always misused when it comes to developing ideas.**

Here is the way brainstorming works. Gather people together, for anywhere between an hour and a couple of days, and generate out-of-the-box ideas. Professional moderators sometimes lead the sessions. Games and mental exercises are usually used to loosen up people's brains.

Our case study on brainstorming is about Bundled Broadband. The idea behind Bundled Broadband was that providers of broadband Internet service—primarily telephone companies and cable television operators—could "bundle" existing and new services together, and collect big basketfuls of cash each month from consumers.

The case of Bundled Broadband is one of the biggest and most expensive mistakes in American business history. Huge companies toppled under the weight of debt created by revenue assumptions that never materialized. Billions in market capitalization were lost as share values in public companies took a nosedive.

American icons like AT&T fell hard. In a feeding frenzy partly driven by the idea of selling bundles of broadband products to Americans, over $100 billion was invested. Large public companies bought and sold cable television systems, bidding the price up from $2,000 a household to $5,000 a household and more. All on the bet that incredible new revenue streams were just around the bend.

Our company in this case study is well-known, but we'll call it NewVision. NewVision, in the middle of the feeding frenzy, decides to jump into bundled broadband.

A group of NewVision employees, suppliers, and partners assembles.

Mission: Brainstorm as many products and services that we can sell to consumers through a broadband pipe. "There are no bad ideas. Go for quantity. Be creative and think outside of the box."

The brainstorming begins. In the beginning, the group produces the obvious ideas:
- Local and long-distance telephone service
- Cable television service
- High-speed Internet service

The first two services have mass appeal, and the third service, high-speed Internet, seemed ready to take off (the time was 2001). In the first hour, the brainstorming group had ideas they thought could entice $150 a month out of consumers' pockets.

The money was already being spent by consumers. All they needed to do was "bundle" the products together, and they could steal market share from the existing suppliers.

Telephone, cable, and Internet were just the beginning:

- How about ordering pizza over your television?
- Educational classes?
- Video dating?
- Ordering groceries from your TV and having them delivered?
- Videoconferencing?
- Video on demand?

Hours passed. The brainstorming group produced hundreds of ideas for products that could be bundled, and sold as a bundle, to families in towns and villages across the country.

Hundreds of ideas! Time to build the pyramid—upside-down.

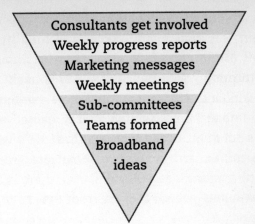

PROBLEM!

Fatal assumption: consumers want bundled services.

The fact is, for the most part customers don't want bundled services. There are very practical reasons. For one, consumers don't like the idea of one big, mega-whopper bill each month, because it makes it hard to budget monthly spending. Another disadvantage is that consumers like to think that companies are competing for their business. Having a single company selling you everything does not feel very competitive.

The moral of the story: hundreds of ideas produced in a brainstorming session do not mean any of them are good. They are the result of a group of businesspeople sitting around. Nobody has asked the consumer yet. Don't be fooled by quantity.

The way to hit new product home runs is to turn the inverse pyramid back upright, so it is sitting flat

on its base, instead of teetering on the top. Instead of assuming you have a good idea and rushing off doing all the work to manufacture or create it, focus your early efforts on the quality of the idea itself. Is the idea really any good, meaning will people buy it in large numbers? It may sound a little theoretical now but it is not at all. In the chapters that follow you will become an expert on the traps and problems with developing new ideas. Following that, there is a simple seven-step process that makes it easy to conquer all of the problems, and to develop ideas and new products that sell!

CHAPTER 5

WHY NINE OUT OF TEN NEW PRODUCTS FAIL

In a world with "business systems" to do everything but polish your car and brush your teeth, the state-of-the-art for developing new ideas lags far, far behind. It's amazing how *little* is written about idea development, and how *little* study has been done on such an important topic. Preparing to write this book, we expected be able to explore other books on the subject. But, in fact, there are none.

- Why should ideas be different than any other business activity?
- What if only one in ten products manufactured was good enough to sell?
- What if only one in ten people we hired were good hires?
- What if only one in ten of our accounting reports was accurate?

- Yet only one in ten ideas succeeds—and that is somehow accepted.
- Every new product or new service starts with an idea.
- Ideas are the *last thing* that should be left to chance!

But they are left to chance. Worse than that, they are left to accepted practices that, more often than not, produce the wrong result.

The key to understanding why nine out of ten new products fail when they get to the marketplace is to understand the tools used to develop new ideas today. Those tools are primarily focus groups, brainstorming, quantitative research, and market segmentation. Some we have discussed, others will be covered for the first time in this chapter. All of these tools and techniques have good and legitimate purposes. But they are often terribly misused when it comes to developing new products. And they are misused even by the "experts." If you learn to recognize how these tools can be misused, that step alone will roughly double your new product success rate.

FOCUS GROUPS

Focus groups are a stalwart of the marketing research trade. For us, researchers who have managed and conducted thousands of groups over twenty-five years, it is embarrassing to tell you the truth.

When it comes to developing ideas:

Most focus groups are a huge waste of time, and as often as not yield an incorrect assessment of what consumers really want.

The focus group process is a ritual. It includes all the elements necessary for a wild ride; a wide mix of junior and senior people traveling to remote cities, tip-of-the-pyramid ideas, advertising agency people and other creative types, and so on.

The feeling at the beginning is giddiness—what will consumers say tonight? Will they like our ideas? Company representatives assemble in a dark back room, behind a one-way mirror. Consumers file in and take their seats, and the group moderator introduces himself. It's showtime!

Over the next several hours, a mini-drama plays out. And it's not what the *consumers* are saying that forms the plot. The drama is unfolding in the back room, where the people from the company sit to observe.

In the back room, the observers munch on M&Ms and pretzels and drink Diet Coke. They talk and try to understand what they are hearing. But this is rarely easy. Here's why:

- **You have eight to ten consumers all talking at once—it's like the Tower of Babel.**
- **Each consumer in the room has a distinct and individual point of view.**
- **But focus groups are meant to get *consensus as quickly as possible,* so we really can't dwell long on what John or Jim or Suzy or Jane meant by that last comment.**

Inevitably, the focus group consumers are saying and wanting different things. But someone in the back room has to draw conclusions, lest the whole night be wasted. Inevitably, the most senior person in the back room throws down the gauntlet:

> "I think what they are really saying is that they want hard-boiled eggs dispensed from ATMs..."

Not wanting to appear stupid or challenging to the boss, everyone in the back room nods in silent agreement. Yes—it's hard-boiled eggs, all right. Still, at the end of the night, there is a need to *really* get closure, so there is often an hour or multi-hour discussion about what consumers said in the preceding four hours (two focus groups at two hours each).

What? Why does it take additional hours to figure out what you have just been listening to for four hours?

> The reason is that focus groups go by too fast. With everyone talking at once, no one can make sense of what is being said.

Think about it: you have eight to ten people, three to eight ideas to show them, and two hours to do it all. Time constraints demand that you "skim the surface," getting sound bites and the only the shallowest of understanding. You also have a more troubling problem:

- **Groups of people are artificial; people rarely make buying decisions in a group.**

- **Consumers certainly do not make buying decisions while discussing that decision in a room full of strangers.**

So you have a time crunch, superficiality in covering the material, and a highly artificial situation. Add to these problems the fact that feedback in focus groups is anything but pure:

- **Participants "cheat" by listening to other participants,**
- **Or give politically correct answers,**
- **Or simply sit mute for two hours to avoid confrontations with other focus group members.**

> ## Focus groups bear some of the burden for the lousy idea success rate in American business.

The chief problem arising from focus groups is a false sense of understanding—thinking you know what people want to buy from you when in reality you have an *entirely artificial result.*

And once an idea gets past the focus group stage in most companies, then gates are opened and the horses are off. You're on your way to developing twenty ideas, hoping to stumble across one that works. Your construction of an upside-down pyramid begins in earnest.

Focus groups are good for some things, but they are not a good way to obtain feedback on concepts or an effective way to evaluate new ideas. After literally thousands of focus groups over many years, it is obvious to us that focus groups yield incorrect answers. Companies do what consumers say they want in focus groups—and the new product or service crashes and burns nine out of ten times.

BRAINSTORMING

Here's another accepted idea development practice that is a cause of American business's disgraceful new-product hit rate. Brainstorming has many legitimate purposes. But when it comes to new products, beware. It is almost universally misused. Here is how brainstorming works. The call is sent out from the castle—bring on some fresh ideas to drive the business!

- **Advertising agency folks and other "creative types" assemble for a brainstorming session.**
- **A few hours are spent trying to unleash the burdens of the day-to-day business and focus on the task at hand.**
- **Between cell phone conversations, fiddling with email, and playing silly games that make everyone uncomfortable...**
- **... a mass of notes are scribbled, and the walls are covered with bits and pieces of "ideas."**

The advice is always the same—go for quantity! There are no bad ideas!

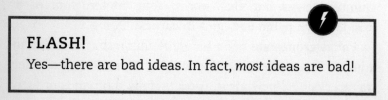

FLASH!
Yes—there are bad ideas. In fact, *most* ideas are bad!

Brainstorming sessions often use mental exercises to get the creative juices flowing, such as:

- "What do you think your dog would say about this pencil if he could talk?"
- "Imagine you are in a huge capsule, floating in space, and the only thing with you is a bright pink lollipop. How would you use that lollipop to sell more term insurance policies?"
- "Everyone—take a newspaper. Close your eyes and blindly point to one word on the page. Now, everyone spend ten minutes thinking about how that word might relate to creating a new spaghetti sauce."

What? You've got to be kidding. It's a wonder that we even have one in ten ideas that succeed!

A successful brainstorming session is almost always measured by the number of discrete thoughts generated. Only a hundred ideas? What a bunch of losers. Several hundred ideas? Getting closer.

It's not uncommon for all-day sessions to "spit up" 1,200 ideas. In one such instance, a major consulting firm had the assignment to brainstorm new ideas. Months were spent carefully cataloging, categorizing, organizing, and otherwise crafting the "master database of ideas." Everybody was mighty proud. The 1,200 ideas were then (somehow) reduced to a dozen, and then finally to five or six that would actually be pursued. Only one idea on the list "succeeded" (marginally) in the end, and it was something the company had already planned to do before the brainstorming session. All the time and money developing ideas was completely wasted.

Any time you hear the words "master database with hundreds of ideas," grab your boots, because you are in for a wild ride, and, usually, a crash landing.

If brainstorming is your company's first step in developing ideas, you are probably wasting your time. Because:

- Brainstorming puts too much emphasis on personal creativity.
- No time is spent doing the time-consuming homework it takes to actually come up with ideas important to the consumer (more on this later).
- It's not the *quantity* of ideas that counts, it's the *quality*.
- Most large organizations (or large brands) can only do one or two major things a year that are new or different. If you try to do more, the result is consumer confusion and poor execution by the unfortunate souls that are trying to keep twenty plates spinning in the air simultaneously.
- Management's job is to find those one or two things that will really make a difference, and ditch the other eighteen things. Ditch the weak ideas that suck brainpower and money out of the organization.

When it comes to ideas, QUALITY COUNTS! As the number of ideas pursued increases, the odds of any one idea being successful declines.

There is nothing wrong with swinging the bat—that is what good business is all about. Business is about risk-taking.

But the way it is done today is incredibly wasteful, and there is a better way. The better way is a seven-step process called Idea Engineering, which will be covered in detail later. For now, we continue to examine the tools that are often misused when developing new products.

QUANTITATIVE RESEARCH

Quantitative research is yet another accepted idea-development practice that is a cause of American business's poor new-product hit rate.

Many large companies take another step after brainstorming and focus groups—quantitative consumer research. This is where you survey hundreds of consumers. This can be a wonderful tool, but unfortunately, it's usually misused in idea development.

> The problem is that, nine times
> out of ten, you do not have
> a strong idea at this point.
> Brainstorming and focus groups
> have led you down a path to failure.

To learn a lot more about a weak idea is not helpful. Or as the icon of modern photography Ansel Adams put it:

"There is nothing worse than a sharp image of a fuzzy concept."

Would you prefer your hard-boiled ATM-dispensed eggs in the shell, or with the shell removed? How much more often will you use our ATMs because of the hard-boiled egg convenience? Would you like salt or pepper with your prepackaged hard-boiled egg? None of these matter since no one wants a hard-boiled egg from an ATM.

Quantitative research on an idea should deliver the most important information, which is revenue potential.

What is this idea worth in old-fashioned revenue?

Later on, we cover exactly how quantitative consumer research can and should be used to *monetize* ideas very early on.

MARKET SEGMENTATION

Market segmentation is cutting up your customer base into groups that have something in common. Then you make products for and/or market specifically to these groups.

All textbooks say this is the thing to do. And, no question, market segmentation has produced some notable successes. Entire industries—like radio and automobiles—are based on segmentation. In many cases, however, we do not feel segmentation is the road you want to follow in order to make a big revenue difference at your company.

A subsequent chapter is fully devoted to market segmentation, but just a quick note about it here. We have conducted, seen conducted, and been a part of dozens of market segmentation efforts. Many of these were a waste of time and money.

The reason is simple. Market segmentation slices and dices the customer base. A new product or service or marketing message directed at these slices, even if it is successful, cannot produce as much revenue as a successful new product or service or marketing message directed at the entire customer base.

Here is the truth:

> If you want to make a big difference, you have a better chance of doing so if you start with something that has the *potential* to be big.

Seems obvious. But over and over again companies lose sight of this while they hunt down tiny markets like left-handed, harmonica-playing, porcelain-doll collectors that eat Twinkies, or something equally as obscure. With the right process, most companies can develop ideas that appeal to their mass audience.

Market segmentation is, in many cases, not the right approach if you want to make big revenue gains. Instead, seek to "aggregate markets"—develop a small number of big ideas that appeal to your entire customer base or to a large portion of that base.

Market segmentation is often an excuse for not developing big ideas that appeal to a company's core customer base. Want proof? Ask anyone who has worked with market segmentations—many, if not most, end up in the trash.

Focus groups, brainstorming, and the rush to segment the customer base—these are some of the reasons the new-idea machine is broken.

> We can and must improve the odds of the ideas we work on.
>
> Business has a moral obligation not to waste *its employees'* time, energy, and enthusiasm.

More and more often, we see the meltdown of entire companies because of a bad idea, or a string of bad ideas. Modern-day management shuffles people around the country, creating armies of employees and their families waiting for their next "tour of duty." Sending armies out with only a 10 percent chance that they are fighting the right battles is not good enough. Great ideas are not a luxury—employees deserve to work on high-odds, high-potential ideas.

Employees are expected to put their hearts and souls into their work, but more often than not they are sent into ratholes to work on ideas that never had a chance, to work on products that won't sell, and to slave over ideas which are simply no good.

> Employees' careers and their families' well-being depend on management's ability to identify great ideas.

CHAPTER 6

HOW A GOOD IDEA CAN GO BAD: THE BATTLE OF THE BAGEL

In the previous chapter we learned why many of the most common idea-development methods that businesses use simply don't work. But while it's nice to know in theory why this doesn't work, it's much more eye-opening to see it happen in real life. So, we'd like to share with you a story from our past that is a great example of why we need to seek a better way.

The Bagel Wars of 1995 are an example of what can go wrong in the idea-development process, and how it can play out in an unfortunate way.

The time was 1995. After lurking in relative obscurity for centuries, the bagel was ready to take its place as the "next big thing" in America. All the indications were there:

- Bagel shops were popping up in towns and cities everywhere.
- Grocery shelves had an ever-growing assortment of prepackaged bagels.

• Big names in breakfast and food (like McDonald's) were jumping in and testing bagels. Not committing, but actively testing and experimenting.

In 1995 the bagel industry was about a $2 billion industry, including bagel shops, grocery stores, and other distribution. The belief was the industry would double in size within five years and become a $5 billion category, and that bagel shops would account for much of the growth. Although there were only twenty-five hundred bagel shops at the time, industry predictions were for as many as ten thousand retail bagel stores. The success of specialty coffee shops like Starbucks further reinforced the belief that consumers' morning habits were shifting away from the fast-feeders to other alternatives. Bagel shops had the chance to participate in the "re-breakfasting" of America.

Bagels were happening!

A seasoned group of managers got the phone call to get a bagel venture rolling. It was Scott Beck making the call—a former Blockbuster Video executive and the CEO and founder of the Boston Market restaurant chain. He was forming a company to attack the bagel market with a string of retail stores across America.

Many of us had worked for Scott at Blockbuster Video during the early days of the video rental business. Blockbuster was the "training ground" for the Bagel Wars. Growth was the name of the game. In our five years at Blockbuster, we opened a store every seventeen hours, seven days a week. The company more than doubled in size, from one thousand to twenty-five hundred plus stores during that time. It was a great business with high margins, a ready audience, and a fun product.

But being involved with a rocket ship like Blockbuster carries its baggage, too—some of us became a little over confident. *Of course* there was luck involved, but weren't we smart, too?

We joined up with the "Bagel Army" in Golden, Colorado. The bagel company was formed by acquiring five bagel specialty chains around the country—the best of the best. Each acquisition was different and each brought specific expertise that could be leveraged to build a national brand. Bagel & Bagel (Kansas City) had incredible store-design talent. Offerdahl's Bagel Gourmet (South Florida) had unique ideas for lighter bagels and lighter whipped cream cheese, and understood how to deliver fast service (critical for morning places). Baltimore Bagel (San Diego) and Brackman Brothers (Salt Lake City) had talented entrepreneurs and know-how. Rounding out the group was Noah's New York Bagels (San Francisco), with a New York deli style look and feel, and an incredibly strong customer following.

Faster than you can say, "I'll have a bagel and a schmear," we had the best bagel operators in the country working to develop a store to roll out nationally—Einstein Brothers Bagels. At the same time, the decision was made to keep one of the acquisitions intact—Noah's New York Bagels—and expand its presence on the West Coast. Einstein-Noah Bagel Corporation was on its way.

It was pretty simple. Scott Beck's plan was to do for the bagel business what had been done in the video rental industry. The plan of attack was to:

- Leverage the wealth of experience from the five bagel-shop acquisitions.

- Raise money in the public markets.
- Create the first nationally branded bagel.
- Take the country by storm by opening lots of units quickly.
- Acquire the very best "fast casual" restaurant real estate in every major market.
- Smoke the tires by executing faster and better than the competition.

Longer term, the hope was to export the branded bagels and cream cheese created by the new entity into other distribution channels, like grocery stores.

It was going to be like the video rental business. Create huge value for shareholders, and in the process, reap rewards for us. A dozen bagels on every table!

But things are not always what they seem to be. American's fascination with bagels was not like their fascination with video rentals, as we would come to learn.

And the restaurant business is a brutal way to make a buck.

Einstein-Noah Bagel Corp. marched ahead. We had a successful IPO, a NYSE listing, acquisitions, accolades, glowing stories in the business press, etc. We went from zero to 350 stores in two years, concentrating mostly on major markets. This rocket was on its way. Everything was just as it should be. A rising stock price gave us the ability to grow quickly.

But there were a couple of problems on the horizon. First and foremost, the company's financial structure was a burden. Early on, sister start-up company Boston Market (operator of Boston Market fast casual restaurants) supplied capital and infrastructure. This early infusion of resources was critical to allowing the fast growth believed necessary to beat competition. If you slowed down, someone else would get the good locations and capture consumers' fancy for bagels.

The financial advantages of having Boston Market as a parent and investor—important early on—became a disadvantage as time progressed. Although Einstein Brothers Bagels had great bagels, cream cheese, and coffee, the company's finances faltered. Einstein Brothers declared Chapter 11, and the rocket ship ride we all hoped for was over just that fast.

The ultimate potential for the bagel business is unknown—financial troubles at Einstein Brothers and elsewhere scorched the category in its infancy. Could bagels have been the next Starbucks? Was there an opportunity to build a business around American's changing breakfast routines? Was there a market for ten thousand bagel shops? It is impossible to tell.

What went wrong? Were bagel stores fundamentally a good idea? Yes. Americans do have something of love affair with the bagel. Ours was a tough lesson about ideas, and about the importance of execution.

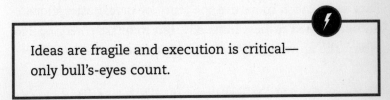

Ideas are fragile and execution is critical—
only bull's-eyes count.

The Bagel Wars are a great example of the need for precision in ideas, and precision in executing those ideas. The company had the right trend and acquired the best operators from which to learn. There was a strong team of managers at headquarters experienced with fast-growth, multi-unit retail. Everything needed was in place. Our mistakes were of a finance and capital structure nature.

The Bagel Wars were a bloodbath for all the players. The competition made different mistakes. One major player had bagel manufacturing equipment in every store, and the cost and complexity was a terrible problem (Einstein-Noah Bagel had centralized bagel production). Other players were under-funded, or had the wrong management team.

At Einstein-Noah Bagel, the most significant mistake, in the always-perfect world of twenty-twenty hindsight, was finances. Specifically, the way the company chose to capitalize and the reliance on sister-company Boston Market. Everything else was executed at a high level by people who knew exactly what they were doing.

Out of the ashes, the bagel industry consolidated, and has continued. Einstein Brothers Bagels and Noah's New York Bagels still exist, part of one of the largest bagel shop chains in the country (New World Restaurant Group operates 630 plus stores in thirty-four states).

If the stars and moon had lined up just a little bit differently, the story of Einstein-Noah Bagel Corporation could have been much more like the story of Blockbuster Video— an unqualified success in its day. But in a fast-emerging category, the growing pains can be immense.

CHAPTER 7

TOP TEN REASONS IDEAS FAIL

In previous chapters, we have given you a brief overview of Idea Engineering—seven repeatable steps to develop ideas that drive business. This chapter focuses on some underlying beliefs that support successful Idea Engineering—beliefs that have helped us develop successful ideas. This chapter explores the ten most common reasons that ideas fail.

Why do the failures help generate new ideas? By studying idea development—both successes and failures, a handful of common themes emerge. Most idea failures fall into one of ten big buckets. Working against these ten shortfalls will make a huge difference in improving your company's odds of success. It's not complicated or fancy. Better idea development boils down to institutionalized common sense.

The Top Ten Reasons Ideas Fail was compiled over two decades by examining hundreds of new product attempts in dozens of different business categories. Be it new food snacks or new consumer electronic products that failed in the market—we began to notice patterns. The same reasons for new product failure kept showing up everywhere, in large companies and small, and in products from corn chips to computers.

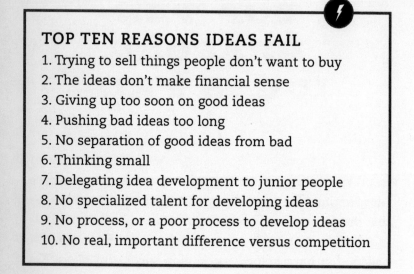

TOP TEN REASONS IDEAS FAIL
1. Trying to sell things people don't want to buy
2. The ideas don't make financial sense
3. Giving up too soon on good ideas
4. Pushing bad ideas too long
5. No separation of good ideas from bad
6. Thinking small
7. Delegating idea development to junior people
8. No specialized talent for developing ideas
9. No process, or a poor process to develop ideas
10. No real, important difference versus competition

REASON #1 IDEAS FAIL: TRYING TO SELL THINGS PEOPLE DON'T WANT TO BUY

America's idea heap is full of stuff people wouldn't buy:
- Transparent jeans
- "New" Coke
- Dot-com anything and everything
- The Weather Radio

This list is long enough for a ninety-volume series. It is the list of things companies have tried to sell people that the people do not want to buy. In many, if not most, of these cases the failures were simply bad ideas.

To be successful with new products it is helpful to understand what failure looks like, and what causes it, in as much detail as possible. Think of this as a forensic idea autopsy, where you are unraveling exactly what went wrong with an idea that resulted in its failure. It is clear to us, based on such forensic idea autopsies on thousands of ideas, that in many cases the end was certain before the game really started. Lack of consumer interest—trying to sell things people don't want to buy—is at the heart of an incredible number of ideas that fail in the marketplace. There is no faster way to tank than trying to sell consumers something they do not want to buy.

Why would any company knowingly spend time and money on ideas with no consumer demand? The answer is simple. To determine if an idea is good or bad, you must predict consumer demand. This is a difficult task, especially for new products.

Better upfront measurement of consumer demand is both possible and critically important. It is possible to predict demand, even at a very early stage of new product development.

> More precision in predicting demand is probably the single most important step you can take to improving your "idea odds."

REASON #2 IDEAS FAIL: THE IDEAS DON'T MAKE FINANCIAL SENSE

Over and over again, idea autopsies show the cause of death to be that "the numbers didn't work."

How is it that companies large and small invest incredible amounts of time, money, and talent into ideas, only to find that, in the end, the numbers don't work? What are people really saying?

Seasoned executives reading this book know the answer. Most often, the mistake can be attributed to an overstatement of gross, top-line revenue.

> Top-line revenue mistakes are unforgivable; they are deadly because top-line revenue drives all the other numbers in financial models.

Whether it is old-fashioned optimism or bad judgment, top-line revenue predictions almost always err on the high side. Most often, the numbers don't work because the idea didn't deliver the expected sales figures.

REASON #3 IDEAS FAIL: GIVING UP TOO SOON ON GOOD IDEAS

There is a finite amount of time large companies will allow for developing and testing new products. The time allowed is often shorter than you would imagine—less than a year in many cases. Then boredom sets in: "It's taking too long so it must be a failure."

You see it over and over again. In large, publicly traded companies, financial pressure drives the following cycle:

- PHASE ONE: Announce plans to develop a new product
- PHASE TWO: Work like the devil on it

- PHASE THREE: Report progress each quarter to Wall Street
- PHASE FOUR: Impatience strikes—what the devil is taking so long?
- PHASE FIVE: Kill it!
- PHASE SIX: Go back to step one and start over again

Wall Street demands growth and performance. Such growth often comes from the launch of new products and services. The Street hates downside surprises. Furthermore, Wall Street rewards current quarter performance. The Street is far less interested in filling the pipeline with good ideas for next year or beyond. Especially as we leave the excesses of the nineties behind, Wall Street is much more about "What have you done for me lately—like in the last fifteen minutes or so?" The only time the Street *really* cares about new products is when you get to a quarter, don't have the new product that you planned on, and miss your numbers. Then, all concerned get a spanking.

Within companies, it is common to see six to nine months allowed for a "new baby" to show serious signs of life. Here, there are also predictable milestones:

- Stage 1: Everyone is excited, kick-off meetings are held, teams formed, budgets established (month one)
- Stage 2: Work and meetings (months two through six)
- Stage 3: We're not getting a heartbeat—dump it (months seven to nine)

When it comes to ideas, *the passage of time* is your enemy.

The practical effect is that, for *whatever* reason, if an idea does not show promise quickly it is often assumed to be a loser. In this Las Vegas-style game of chance where ten or twenty hands are played in the hope of one winner, you must cut your losses quickly. There is not enough time or money to fund all development efforts.

Here's a tragedy: under the time pressure, it is often the *very best* ideas that are thrown out. Why? The most powerful ideas, in terms of driving huge revenue gains, are usually the hardest to figure out and execute.

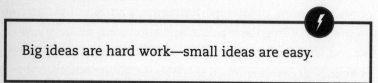

Big ideas are hard work—small ideas are easy.

Companies often think it is better to cut losses and focus on those things that are showing promise—usually the ideas that are easy and quick to execute and almost always low level and of less value. The problem: if it's easy for you, it'll be easy for your competitor to copy.

REASON #4 IDEAS FAIL: PUSHING BAD IDEAS TOO LONG

This is a close cousin to giving up on good ideas too soon. Interestingly, both of these mistakes are often made for the same reason, which is:

> Companies pursue bad ideas too long because they are, almost always, the easiest, lowest risk, and most conservative.

Companies pursue bad ideas too long because they can *actually see progress,* and reach a conclusion. Finishing something makes everyone feel good. Never mind that when you are done you have not put much money in the cash register.

Big ideas that can drive breakthrough gains in profitable revenue are almost always *very different.* Consider companies formed around simple yet very different ideas, like:

- eBay—turning the obscure, small-time auction business into a world marketplace
- Federal Express—overnight package delivery
- Wal-Mart—built from the ground up to support low prices
- Southwest Airlines—skip the frills, but get people to their destination on time for a value, and lighten their day with a touch of fun

None of the companies here, with their breakthrough business models, were overnight successes. Consider how long personal computers and the Internet was around before eBay showed up. Or consider that Wal-Mart opened its first unit in Rogers, Arkansas, in 1962. It took Wal-Mart seventeen years to reach a billion dollars in sales annually, which is not a particularly big number for a retailer. Or how long it took to perfect the ultimate simplicity of Southwest Airlines' no frills, fast-gate-turnaround model that represents a new breed of airline service. Federal Express delivered their first 186 packages, using fourteen small planes, in 1973. What is the prize for being patient? Wal-Mart sees one hundred million shoppers every week. Southwest Airlines was the only airline that remained profitable after 9/11. In the online auction world, eBay leads and has a market capitalization of $50 billion as of this writing. Federal Express stands for overnight package delivery.

There is another reason that breakthrough ideas are hard to foster, while the easy (but low-value) ideas move ahead. Large organizations appeal to employees who are risk-averse, as large firms offer more stability. The rank-and-file in *Fortune* companies are there because they have chosen not to be entrepreneurs, or take undue risks with their careers. That's fine, because most of the work in large organizations requires exactly that kind of mindset. In big, successful companies, the first priority is to protect and maintain the core business.

But when it comes to ideas, there is a different need. We need to teach a *better process* for developing big ideas that people can understand and use. We need a process that enables people who are doing a stellar job in every other part of modern corporations to do a stellar job in developing new ideas.

In today's corporate environment, small ideas are encouraged and big ideas are discouraged. The result is that we give up on good ideas too soon, and push bad ideas too long.

REASON #5 IDEAS FAIL: NO SEPARATION OF GOOD IDEAS FROM BAD

One of the toughest business problems is deciding which new product or service initiatives should get money and manpower. It's a brutal problem where incorrect decisions cost careers or make heroes.

There is never a shortage of possibilities, as ideas percolate up from every nook and cranny. The killer is figuring out which ideas have the most potential. Today, finance and marketing folks are usually charged with estimating the revenue and costs of developing discrete ideas. They do their best, but the reality is that *most of what gets approved ends up tanking in the marketplace* (one out of ten ideas succeed).

Is it just bad ideas? No. As our old friend and marketing whiz Jim Hilmer says, there are two requirements for business success—Great Ideas and Great Execution (we have Hilmer to thank for the phrase "lightning in a bottle," which he shared with us in 1993). A good idea poorly executed is still a failure. But bad ideas account for at least half and probably far more of all idea failures in America. Fix the quality of ideas, and immediately see a doubling in your successful idea percentages.

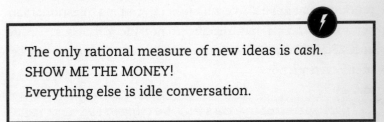

The only rational measure of new ideas is *cash.*
SHOW ME THE MONEY!
Everything else is idle conversation.

In order to separate the good ideas from the bad, you must develop sound, realistic measures of what ideas are worth to *consumers.* How many of what you want to sell will they buy? How much will they spend if your new product is available? This is not a *guess* on revenue from marketing folks, or finance, or operations. *You need to measure the value of ideas while they are in the concept stage* (i.e., before a lot of money has been spent). **Monetize** your ideas.

REASON #6 IDEAS FAIL: THINKING SMALL

It seems like the larger and more mature the company, the more likely they are to fall into the **Segmentation Trap**.

- You start with a large, successful business, selling things to a large, mass market.
- New ideas are developed to appeal to the same audience, following the Las Vegas odds for new product ideas that only one in ten succeed.
- Somebody—usually the advertising agency or marketing folks, suggests a new approach—**segmentation**.

A segmentation strategy usually makes sense on the surface—take small slices of your customer base and make products that appeal to each of them. And, no question, market segmentation has produced notable successes. Entire industries, like radio and automobiles, are based on market segmentation.

> But, in many cases, segmentation is not the road you want to take, if you want to produce large revenue gains.

Here's why. In any situation, it's hard to do ten things at once, and do them well. But in a large company, it is hard to do *one* big thing well! While there are exceptions, like Procter & Gamble, which can pull off multiple successes, most large companies can grow by doing one or two big things extremely well (e.g., Dell expanding beyond computers to home electronics).

By thinking small and segmenting markets, you end up with a large number of ideas. A lot of things may get done, but none of them get done especially well, and few (one in ten) amount to much in the way of profitable revenue. The inevitable result is pure mediocrity.

Our experience is that **it is better to have one big idea that appeals to your mass market**—the customers who know and love you—than ten small ideas that each appeal to a small sliver of customers

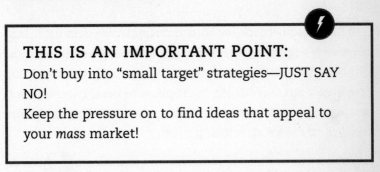

THIS IS AN IMPORTANT POINT:
Don't buy into "small target" strategies—JUST SAY NO!
Keep the pressure on to find ideas that appeal to your *mass* market!

Is it harder to find idea that appeals to your mass market? No, not if you use the seven steps outlined for Idea Engineering.

Chapter 9 expands on how to avoid the small idea trap. You can vastly improve your idea odds by heading 180 degrees away from the *segmentation trap*—instead, use the principle of market *aggregation*. Seek a single idea that appeals to your mass customer base (aggregation), and avoid splitting your business into tiny little buckets that require individual care and feeding (segmentation).

REASON #7 IDEAS FAIL: DELEGATING IDEA DEVELOPMENT TO JUNIOR PEOPLE

Who is in charge of developing ideas at your company? If your company is like many others, the job falls to junior people. Do you have a senior person whose job depends on seeking big, new ideas, and readying them for the market? Most companies do not.

Who is in charge of developing ideas at your company—who gets fired if they fail?

The responsibility for idea development often falls into marketing—specifically, market research. Research is a vital and valuable function and can be a huge help in developing new ideas, but it is *not* the right place to create and develop new ideas. Consumer and market research talent is not the same as talent for developing ideas.

> Traditional market research is often a poor location to place your bets for big ideas.

Profitable growth comes from big ideas. Finding and advocating big ideas is hard, dangerous work. Ideas that are going to drive the needle big-time are going to require significant change.

Idea development requires senior level involvement—period.

REASON #8 IDEAS FAIL: NO SPECIALIZED TALENT FOR DEVELOPING IDEAS

Why is it that the single most important growth driver—new ideas—has so little specialized talent devoted to it? Why aren't there dozens of "idea factories" with "idea experts," all attacking what is such an obvious opportunity of turning one in ten odds into one in five odds, or one in three?

The typical cost to develop an idea is $1 to 3 million dollars. (Note: For a large company, $3 mil is the typical cost to get to a prototype situation, but the costs can run ten or twenty times higher than that.) That means there is an awful lot of money going down the bad-idea rat hole. Why is there so little specialized talent for developing ideas?

It is a true mystery. The lack of expertise and sound processes for developing successful new products is baffling, and is what motivated this book.

REASON #9 IDEAS FAIL: NO PROCESS, OR A POOR PROCESS, FOR DEVELOPING IDEAS

This is blasphemy, you say! Of *course* there is a process for developing great ideas at my company! Here's a surprise—senior management's fervor for developing successful new products wanes quickly as you move down the ranks. There are a number of very valid reasons why.

"Been there, done that." The rank and file understands the one in ten odds. They have been down enough idea rat holes not to get too excited by the next one that gets passed along. There isn't a good process that assures good ideas at the back end, and the rank and file knows it.

In terms of effort, working on new ideas is, in general, a bad job—you are working at 10 percent efficiency. It's exhausting. Most everything you do is, literally, a waste of time. To the troops, your hot new widget is just another item on a to-do list that is plenty full already, thank you.

The trick is to *institutionalize* the commitment to develop great ideas. Stop accepting one in ten idea odds.

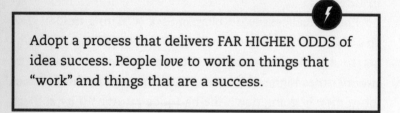

Adopt a process that delivers FAR HIGHER ODDS of idea success. People *love* to work on things that "work" and things that are a success.

Give folks that opportunity by clearing out the loser ideas early on, and focusing on a small number of big winners!

It is pretty simple—whoever is responsible for company growth *must* be the idea champion...*must* adopt a process to improve idea odds...*must* use that process to institutionalize a commitment to develop great ideas.

REASON #10 IDEAS FAIL: NO REAL, IMPORTANT DIFFERENCE VERSUS COMPETITION

It is not easy to find something important and different to consumers in this day and age; truly, we have access to an awful lot of products.

Motorola is a fine company that brought U.S. business incredible advances in manufacturing quality, along with a ton of other technological advancements. In the early eighties, it was really an engineer's paradise.

To engineering folks, the patent is the Holy Grail. And Motorola earned plenty of them, and made boatloads of money from everything from walkie-talkies to remote telemetry for ambulances to the first cellular telephones. But there were also some big mistakes.

In our days as new product planners with Motorola, the (lowly) marketers covertly referred to the problem as the Gee Whiz! factor, or "falling in love with your own idea." The problem was confusing something new and different with something that consumers would want to purchase.

After literally inventing cellular telephones and owning the cell phone market in the early years, Motorola later stumbled. The company was slow to see the switch from the older analog systems to newer digital phones that offered more features that consumers wanted. Analog cell phone technology was what brought Motorola to the party—and the company was slow on the trigger to embrace the new, better digital systems. The company had fallen in love with their original way of doing things, and it hurt them for some time, as competitors beat them to the market with rich-featured digital cell phones.

BE MORE SUCCESSFUL BY UNDERSTANDING WHY IDEAS FAIL

In the end, all that matters is will your idea make the cash register ring. Low tech. High tech. Whatever. Figure out exactly what your consumers want that the competition is not offering; this is the heart of your new idea engine.

So that is it. The Top Ten Reasons Ideas Fail. Want to make a world of improvement in your idea odds? Stop accepting Las Vegas odds of one in ten. Attack the problem with a *process* that works. *Institutionalize* the commitment to new ideas by being the cheerleader for a better way, and *kill loser ideas* that sap energy out of your organization.

CHAPTER 8

LESS IS MORE

When it comes to developing new ideas....

LESS IS MORE

- "Less Ideas" Is More.
- "Less People" Is More.
- "Less Words" Is More.

This chapter focuses on specific steps that can be taken to dramatically unleash new idea creativity, and get more good ideas with less time, people, and effort.

The thoughts expressed are 180 degrees opposite from conventional wisdom. But conventional wisdom brought American business to where it is today—with far too many failed ideas and far too few ideas that really drive the growth. Let's look at how to change this.

"LESS IDEAS" IS MORE

The #1 fallacy about ideas is that you need a lot of ideas in order to end up with business success. Nothing could be further from the truth.

That twisted belief is based on the notion that the best way to get a good idea is to start with a boatload of ideas, which, by definition, are *mostly* bad, and then try to sort through the huge pile of coal and find a diamond. It is a ridiculous approach, it doesn't work, and it is a leading cause for the grim success rate of ideas in America.

> The #1 fallacy in the idea business is that you need *a lot* of ideas in order to end up with a success. *Nothing* could be further from the truth.

In the end, even giant organizations need only one to three really big ideas a year. Why? Because large organizations can only execute a few large initiatives at one time.

> Working on too many ideas at once results in *everything* being done at a C level.

Working on too many ideas makes it hard to recognize a success. The trick is to identify which one to three ideas will dramatically drive profitable revenue. Then trash all other ideas that get in the way of those few things that can really make a difference.

> ## You simply need a few really good consumer-focused ideas that will allow you to efficiently drive revenue.

"Less ideas" is more. Said another way, it is better to have a few really good ideas than a ton of mediocre ones.

"LESS PEOPLE" IS MORE

Everyone has seen this strange phenomenon. Given the same task, a small handful of people run circles around a large group. And this is particularly true when developing new ideas.

> More often than not, too many people working on idea development has the opposite effect of what is desired.

More resources usually *add* time to a task rather than reduce the time.

> The more resources you put against doing something, the more time it takes.

Why? One factor is the added permutations and combinations of communication streams. Small teams can pretty much manage communication between themselves. The communications in larger groups increase in logarithmic fashion.

One thing is for certain; the larger the group on a task, the larger the meetings. And then "meeting math" kicks in. In a small group, say five people, everyone can have their say and you can still cover a lot of real work in an hour.

With twenty people in a meeting, there is barely time to get through everyone's opening remarks, monologues, and other updating and speechmaking before the hour is over, and you haven't gotten anything of substance accomplished.

Now, add interdepartmental coordination and squabbles and the reality that today's employees are juggling more tasks than they ever have, and are having a hard time focusing on any single thing.

> Large new product development teams are notoriously inefficient and slow.

Developing powerful ideas that can drive significant revenue gains may start with a sizable team of people. But the team size should quickly be pared to a small number.

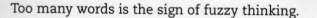

When it comes to developing new ideas, the best model is "A Few Good Men and Women."

"LESS WORDS" IS MORE

Both Mark Twain and Albert Einstein are credited with the saying, "I would have written a shorter letter, but did not have the time."

They mean, of course, that brevity takes time.

Too many words is the sign of fuzzy thinking.

One of the most talented idea people we had the opportunity to work with was Mark Goldston. Goldston's credits included stints as president and COO at L.A. Gear, CMO at Reebok, and president of Faberge USA, Inc., as well as an inventor-of-record on numerous separate U.S. patents. Goldston, author of *The Turnaround Prescription,* further proved his prowess in the world of big ideas by taking a tiny, fledgling dot-com hopeful called NetZero, saving it from the doom that destroyed so many dot-com businesses in the 1990s, and in short measure turning it into the second largest (and most profitable) Internet service provider in the world by 2004.

When reporting to the colorful and talented Goldston at Einstein-Noah Bagel Corp., at the end of any consumer research the most important thing was a clear, unambiguous action item. He was interested in the details that supported your conclusion, but at the end of a discussion, a succinct recommendation was what really mattered.

It did not make any difference that the briefing was the result of an incredibly complex study of food chemistry for making the "perfect bagel," or the results of a consumer study that would dramatically influence the design of our stores. What mattered was a specific, actionable recommendation based on the data. One of Goldston's favorite sayings to me was, "You say it, and I'll swear to it." It was his way of saying, "I've listened to you carefully, and I'm counting on you to be right."

How do these actionable recommendations work? One example is when the company faced a huge challenge early on: how do you make one, standardized bagel that will satisfy palates across the country? Months and months of consumer taste tests had been conducted. It all came down to a single bagel recipe that was unlike any existing bagel, but had many of the common elements that consumers liked in a bagel—chewy but not too chewy, a bit of crackle when you bite it, etc. The risk was high. Going with a single bagel for the whole country would save money and allow for fast expansion. Being wrong entailed a potentially fatal risk for the company. Would it work? The months of consumer research and taste tests said yes. The CEO believed it, and we did it. The one country, one bagel strategy worked.

Goldston, like most successful CEOs we've worked with, used consumer research to identify very specific actions that could make a difference. No wordiness, no fuzziness. No learning for learning's sake. While the ultimate size of the bagel business was a disappointment for all of us, as mentioned previously, Goldston went on to wow the online world as chairman, CEO, and president of United Online, which through organic growth, acquisition, and sheer entrepreneurial talent became one of the largest and most profitable Internet service providers in the world (brands include NetZero and Juno).

Take a page from the great CEOs we've known like Mark Goldston. Think about how less can be more in your business or job. Even if you are not always right—and no one is—distinguish yourself by being clear and succinct when it comes to new product opportunities and risks. At the same time, be ready to for the heat that comes with cutting to the chase.

> ## Being brief is scary—saying what you think in a succinct manner leaves very little room for wiggling.

Be different! The world is full of people who are risk averse, and prefer muddling to crystal-clear communications. Don't be one of them.

Complicated ideas, along with the use of technical language or business lingo is a fog created to make it sound like you know what you are doing even when you don't. There are two reasons this is so common; (1) to avoid being trapped by specifics, and (2) because you are not clear in your own mind of you want to say.

Hey, everyone's used this writing style at one time or another—but it's to be staunchly avoided when writing stuff that you want normal humans to understand.

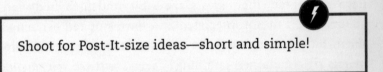

Shoot for Post-It-size ideas—short and simple!

The best ideas, like the best advertising, are written in a brief, "kindergarten simple" fashion. Here's why: Americans are exposed to a huge volume of advertising every day via television, radio, the Internet, stores, billboards, and on and on. You need to get to their brains lightning fast to make an impact.

Good ideas—the ones that will drive the business—are incredibly simple to understand. People "get" them almost instantaneously. Good advertising conveys a good idea so that the consumer instantly gets it. Advertising is simply expression of an idea that has floated further downstream.

Consumers have developed an amazing defense mechanism for dealing with the daily, neverending flood of messages trying to sell them something—they simply tune out. They don't listen unless the message is instantly clear and understandable.

Our belief about the importance of message brevity comes from listening to hundreds of consumers react to thousands of ideas, and thousands of advertising messages. As you watch, you realize these people are giving you about three seconds to get your message across—that's it. If you don't hit a nerve in three seconds, anything and everything else you say is completely useless.

And this is in a setting where you are interviewing consumers one at a time in a conference room. They are being paid to listen to what you are presenting. Even in this setting, if folks do not hear something of *real interest* in the first sentence they read, their eyes glaze a bit, and their body language says "I'm not interested and have stopped listening." Everything and anything else you show them after that point means zip—nada, zero, nothing. *They have tuned you out, and you haven't gotten to the "good stuff" yet!*

In the course of observing such one-on-one interviews over many years, it has become very clear that:

> Ideas have to sizzle in the first three seconds, or forget it.

The level of consumer engagement for new products and services is nothing short of frightening. Consumers don't simply reject you "for cause." Consumers reject you before you barely open your mouth. They reject you if you haven't made your point in three seconds. Literally.

It has become so predicable over the years that we just refer to it in shorthand: The Three-Second Rule. In communicating ideas, there isn't *time* to be wordy; there's barely time to say the most important thing you need to say.

The solution is brevity and relevance. You have three seconds, that's it. You must say *exactly* what will make consumers want to buy your product, and you must get their attention in the first three seconds (roughly one short sentence).

Consumers *will* listen beyond three seconds, but only if you get their attention in the early, critical seconds. Management guru Peter Drucker said it like this: "The aim of marketing is to know and understand the customer so well the product or service fits him and *sells itself.*"

Nowhere is the need for brevity and relevance more important than in today's world of ideas of new products and services.

Don't follow the crowd. The crowd is tanking when it comes to pushing out high odds ideas that drive dramatic business results. Focus on less:

- **Less Ideas**—to clog the development and execution pipeline
- **Less People**—tripping over themselves in developing new ideas
- **Less Words**—make your idea sizzle in three seconds

These simple principles, followed with a vengeance, will double or triple your organization's idea success rate.

simply reject you "for cause." Consumers reject you before you barely open your mouth. They reject you if you haven't made your point in three seconds. Literally.

It has become so predicable over the years that we just refer to it in shorthand: The Three-Second Rule. In communicating ideas, there isn't *time* to be wordy; there's barely time to say the most important thing you need to say.

The solution is brevity and relevance. You have three seconds, that's it. You must say *exactly* what will make consumers want to buy your product, and you must get their attention in the first three seconds (roughly one short sentence).

Consumers *will* listen beyond three seconds, but only if you get their attention in the early, critical seconds. Management guru Peter Drucker said it like this: "The aim of marketing is to know and understand the customer so well the product or service fits him and *sells itself*."

Nowhere is the need for brevity and relevance more important than in today's world of ideas of new products and services.

Don't follow the crowd. The crowd is tanking when it comes to pushing out high odds ideas that drive dramatic business results. Focus on less:

- **Less Ideas**—to clog the development and execution pipeline
- **Less People**—tripping over themselves in developing new ideas
- **Less Words**—make your idea sizzle in three seconds

These simple principles, followed with a vengeance, will double or triple your organization's idea success rate.

CHAPTER 9

MARKET SEGMENTATION AND AGGREGATION

When it comes to new products, there is a fork in the road early on that leads either one direction or the other. The first path is developing products that appeal to a large target audience. The second path is to develop a more niche product, or something that appeals to a smaller target audience. Targeting a smaller market is known as market segmentation. Targeting a large market is known as mass marketing, or aggregation.

Aggregation is often a much better way to develop new products. The best way to understand the power of aggregation is to first consider the opposite, which is market segmentation.

Market segmentation has its place in the marketer's toolbox. However, the technique is often grossly misused, resulting in new products that fail. Because market segmentation is so common a technique and so commonly misused, we cover it first.

MARKET SEGMENTATION: THE BASICS

This section explores market segmentation—what it is, why it's around, and how it *really* works. And most importantly, this chapter covers:

> ### Why segmenting markets can be an enemy if your career depends on driving big revenue gains.

First: what is market segmentation?

"The managerial concept underlying market segmentation is the identification of a group of consumers who have needs or responses that are different from other consumers. A product intended for the total market may have only marginal success if consumers have different perspectives."
—Glen Urban and John Hauser, *Design and Marketing of New Products,* 2nd Edition, 1993

"Segmenting markets is widely accepted as one of the requirements for successful marketing. By dividing the market into relatively homogenous submarkets, both strategy formulation and tactical decision-making (e.g., the choice of media for advertising) can be simplified."
—Donald Lehmann, *Market Research and Analysis,* 1989

Most marketing books include market segmentation as one of the Ten Commandments of marketing. It has been taught in business schools so long that nobody questions it or thinks twice about the benefits of segmenting markets.

And market segmentation is not just a lowly marketing commandment—it is up near the top of the list. Segmentation is presented as the Mercedes of marketing tools, the gold standard for use by big, sophisticated, high-power firms that are taking their marketing to the next level.

Everyone has heard of market segmentation. Most folks believe in it. We believe, however, that:

> **Market segmentation—specifically the computer-driven variety—often fails when it comes to driving large, profitable revenue gains.**

First, however, a qualification. We agree that some forms of what is loosely referred to as market segmentation have produced notable successes. In fact there are whole industries based entirely on market segmentation (radio and automobiles, for instance).

The typical large market has a radio station for every musical taste—'70s to alternative to pop to country to classical. Automobile manufactures produce a variety of cars and trucks for different budgets, ages, tastes, or styles.

Another clear success where a form of market segmentation works extremely well is the field of direct, or database, marketing. Indeed, marketing to small groups, or even individuals, based on what they buy continues to grow, and often produces excellent results. Also, it is often useful to think about your business with an eye to some kind of grouping to decide who is, and who isn't, a target.

The kind of market segmentation situation we are talking about, the one that doesn't work, is different. It happens when you are in a company with a reasonably broad market. And, faced with coming up with new ideas to drive revenue, somebody says, "We need to do a computer-driven segmentation of our customers and tailor our new product ideas to the segments."

What they mean is a "sophisticated," computer-driven segmentation. If you say yes to one of these, you are, far more times than not, on the road to failure. Here is how it happens...

We are research directors for a Fortune 500 company. At the request of the chief marketing officer, whose neck is on the line for coming up with new ideas to drive the business, we do a computer-driven market segmentation study—a massive market-research project spanning several months, and hundreds of thousands of dollars in cost. Finally, the study is done and now it's time for the results.

Since targeting strategies can affect everything you are doing in marketing, everyone and his brother needs to hear the results—staff marketing personnel, ad agency people, pricing gurus, promotional agency representatives, and so on. The first presentation includes a dozen key people.

The meeting is held off-site at a beautiful beachfront hotel. Off-site meetings are big-company code for "something really special is happening here." This is not a place for "average" thoughts.

The "expert" from the market research company that conducted the computer-driven segmentation study stands at the front of the room. He talks about methodological issues. Eyes glaze. People reach for their coffee and fiddle with their cell phones. All anyone wants to hear is the result. Drum roll please. "Using cluster analysis, we have identified these six, distinct targets: they are as follows...."

The initial reaction in the room is nervous excitement, almost giddiness. The reaction is: "Wow—who would have ever thought THAT!" The six target segments are presented. Each has a clever name meant to make the segments come to life. Names like "Time-Stressed Urban Couch Potatoes" and "Technology-Advanced Weekend Warriors."

The presentation of the data lasts several hours. Then it is time to make hay. "Our goal now is to develop separate strategies for each of the individual segments." So we talk about how we might be able to do that. And talk and talk. And then talk some more.

The chief marketing officer tells us we need to end up with four to six market segments to which we can advertise in a targeted manner. Marketing spending will be $200 million for the next year, about the same as this year, but we will have tailored marketing campaigns for each of the four to six segments. Each segment will get a piece of the $200 million. He expects business results to be better because marketing will be better targeted.

> By the end of the day, it is clear, according to our discussion so far, that there is neither the money nor the time to market to four to six different market segments.

Two weeks later, same meeting room, same beachfront hotel, but now we have twice the number of attendees. Anybody that might have a clue about how to market to all the tiny market segments we created is invited. It's the same presentation. And then, drum roll, please! "We have identi-fied these six, distinct targets: they are as follows…"

Another day is spent trying to develop six "mini-marketing campaigns" (for the price of the one large campaign used before). Another day ends with exhaustion and an unpleasant conclusion by the chief marketing officer: "Something is wrong."

The spankings begin. The CMO wants to know what is screwed up—how come this isn't working? Computer-driven market segmentation works—everybody does it. Why is it not working here?

Here is why it is not working. First, segmentation studies often yield segments that are based on what are called psy-chographic variables/profiles (and that is the case here). But you can't buy media or advertise based on psychographic profiles. For all intents and purposes, media is sold based on demographics. So there is no way to advertise to these artifi-cial, computer-generated groups of people—there is simply no way to reach them.

The second problem is money. You can't reach four to six different groups, with different messages, for the same money as advertising one message to a single, mass audi-ence.

> You can't develop six separate marketing campaigns for the price of one.

And the segmentation, like most computer-driven seg-mentation studies, f-a-d-e-s away.

We were involved with this example. We have been involved with others. Too many of the segmentations we have been involved with and have heard about ended up like the case study above. Initial excitement, followed by a growing sense of disappointment, followed by fade to black.

Most organizations, even very large ones, lack the money to *really* get their "story" out. Consumers, faced with an ever-increasing barrage of advertising, are tuning out. So it takes more and more money and time to communicate even the simplest of notions.

> If you want to market to six discrete segments—you either need six times the money, or you must divide up the money you are spending now and spend one-sixth the money on each segment.

A critical mistake that we see over and over again is going after market segments that are too small. Instead of growing the revenue pie, computer-driven segmentations too often result in taking your big pie and splitting it into a number of small pieces. Make sure any market opportunity that you attack is big enough to support your time and effort. This seems obvious, but is often overlooked.

Here is another dirty little secret.

> Computer-driven market segmentation is a figment of your imagination.

"The first thing to recognize is that market segmentation is usually a figment of a researcher's or a manager's imagination. While customers are different, a particular segmentation scheme is one of an infinite number that could be created."
—Donald Lehmann, *Market Research and Analysis,* 1989

Without knowing the statistics, upper management seems to sense this. The decision to abandon segmented marketing therefore becomes easy; management does not believe the segments, and there's no money to support all of that extra effort anyway.

Here is yet another problem with segmentation. By design, market segmenting generates *more* efforts and ideas, not *less.*

Most large companies or brands do not need more ideas—they need a few ideas that really make the tires burn.

As discussed in chapter 8, when it comes to ideas, less is more.

In a way, the computer-driven segmenting of markets is like throwing in the towel. It says, "We can't think of a *mass-market proposition* that would appeal to our whole customer base, so we'll carve our customer base into a bunch of tiny pieces." And too often the pieces are too small to be a viable business, or are simply artificial and not actionable. The assumption is that a bunch of tiny pieces will be easier to attack. It sounds good, but doesn't work.

So, if market segmentation is so flawed, what should you do instead?

Read on.

AGGREGATION: THE KEY TO THE NEW PRODUCT VAULT

If segmenting markets is not the road you want to take to create big revenue gains, what should you do?

> Focus instead on AGGREGATION!

Instead of segmentation, put your marketing and new-product efforts behind ideas that will appeal to the largest possible audience. You need one-size-fits-all ideas that appeal in a big way to the vast majority of your customer base.

Large successful companies have an incredible advantage in the quest for big ideas. A large number of customers already know and love your products. That is how you got big to begin with. They *want* to do business with you—all you need to do is continue to give them reasons to stick. Give them a good reason, and they will give you more love!

One big idea that appeals to almost everybody is—90 percent of the time—worth more than a basketful of ideas that appeal to smaller parts of your customer base.

Does this strategy of aggregation work? You bet, and the reason is common sense 101:

> If you want to make a big difference, then start with something big!

Segmentation strategies, by definition, ask that you start with something small. Marketing to specific groups sometimes makes sense. Such targets are usually *very obvious* and don't require complicated analysis to identify—common sense and simple business judgment will point you in the right direction.

Aggregation is just the opposite. Aggregation says that you "mass up" your customer base and find something that all your customers want to buy from you. You will almost always be rewarded by ignoring the urge to carve your customer base into segments—segments that amount to "needy little buckets"—and instead, focusing on aggregation.

Let's say you have a company doing $5 billon a year in sales. Your goal is to increase revenue 15 percent. If you start with something big—your entire customer base—a single idea can be developed and executed that will drive $750 million in incremental revenue.

> Contrary to popular belief, single ideas with revenue potential of 15 percent or more can almost always be developed, even in mature, large businesses.

Here's why. The way big companies got big in the first place was by having one good idea that appealed to a *lot* of people; ideas like:

- Starbucks—a great way to start the day or an afternoon treat
- Wal-Mart—"always low prices"
- Disney—family fun

With most of the companies above, it took only one idea to bring them to the party. And as the all-star list above seek to grow their businesses—they look to a *small number* of new ideas that appeal to their mass audience.

- Starbucks—added light food to compliment the coffee
- Wal-Mart—built stores in non-traditional neighborhoods
- Disney—multiply the opportunities to access the brand, like Disney Cruises

Especially if you already have a large consumer franchise, your best strategy is to:

> **Harness the masses that already love you—and give them a new and/or better way to do business with you.**

Let's see how this compares to segmentation. Say you decide to segment your market. You end up with five segments. To drive revenue 15 percent, you now need *five* big ideas. And each idea must drive a 15 percent revenue gain against their intended target/segment. Which is easier, rallying the troops around a single idea that applies to your mass customer base, or around five ideas?

Yet time and again, companies skip the lower-hanging fruit of a single idea and head down the path of developing five small ideas—each of which requires time and money, and each of which has to work in order to get the whole revenue base to advance 15 percent.

Is it a surprise that America's biggest companies have to do ten or twenty things to find one that works? No. Given the toolbox full of disasters like computer-driven market segmentations, it's a surprise the odds aren't worse than they are.

What's the message, then?

> Don't be fooled by fancy marketing schemes that use computers to replace common sense. Develop ideas that aggregate your customers—not separate them. Don't let anyone talk you into segments that are unaffordable and artificial.

Think in terms of one-size-fits-all, and don't let lazy thinking get you off track for the big prize—a *single idea* that can smoke the tires!

CHAPTER 10

THE CREATIVE GENIUS OF TED TURNER AND RUPERT MURDOCH

There are idea people who change the world with great intuitive leaps—ideas so new and radically different that they seem to have come out of nowhere. These people have a gift—creative genius.

Most of us are not creative geniuses. So having a system with which to *create* and *develop* ideas—a system which requires some creativity but relies just as much on mental elbow grease—is a help for the rest of us.

Although creative geniuses live in a world of their own and the way they come up with ideas is, to some degree, beyond our ability to comprehend, it is still helpful to study these people. By doing so, we can pick up some pointers as to how we can create and develop our own ideas.

In this chapter, we take a look at a couple of creative geniuses from the media world—Ted Turner and Rupert Murdoch. We pick these two because they are, in fact, creative geniuses and because they are both colorful and controversial figures. Most of us have watched their programs, read their newspapers, or are customers in some other way of these creative geniuses.

TED TURNER

Turner is not just a business giant, but also an American legend. He revolutionized broadcasting, won the America's Cup, owned a baseball team that won the World Series, started the Goodwill Games, pledged $1 billion to the United Nations for humanitarian causes, became the largest land owner in America, and, last but not least, married Jane Fonda. His net worth in 2005 is about $2 billion, down from roughly $8 billion when he sold Turner Broadcasting to Time Warner.

Turner took over the family billboard business at age twenty-five, after his father committed suicide. It was the largest billboard business in the South and in reasonably good shape. But the pressures of running the business were partially responsible for Turner's father taking his own life.

Ted Turner showed early on just how brilliant a businessman he was by quickly putting the business in order and expanding it dramatically. And he did it on a part-time basis. He spent at least half his time racing sailboats.

In 1970, Turner, against the strong counsel of all his advisors, bought an Atlanta UHF television station that was hemorrhaging money. At the time, fewer than half the TV sets in Atlanta could pick up UHF (as some of you may remember, to pick up UHF back then you had to have a special set of rabbit ears sitting on top of the television). Everybody who worked at Turner Broadcasting thought the station would take the entire company down.

> **LESSON #1:** Creative business geniuses see the future.

Turner bought it because he could see the future and the future was TV. He wanted in because he figured a TV license would dramatically appreciate in value, regardless of how poor a property it was to begin with. Creative business geniuses see the future.

> **The more we—you and I—can visualize and anticipate the future, the better our ideas will be.**

For us, seeing the future means putting in the time—doing your learning on a full-time basis.

An asset, however much it might be worth in the future, is not worth much now if it is hemorrhaging money. So Turner's first job was to create value in something that had little value. And he did it very quickly, again on a part-time basis. Turner was, at the time, a serious sailor with world-class skills. In fact, he was the best in the world, winning Yachtsman of the Year four times and the America's Cup in 1977.

Turner added value by programming the station himself—with a combination of cartoons, old black-and-white movies, 1950s' series reruns like *Leave It to Beaver* and *Lassie,* professional wrestling, and Atlanta Braves' baseball games. Viewers liked the combination of programming enough to move WTCG to 15 percent of the audience, unheard of for a UHF station. By 1973, three years after Turner acquired the station, it was making $1 million a year.

> **LESSON #2:** Creative business geniuses know what the public wants.

Turner has a connection with the man and woman in the street, the people who come home at night and turn on their televisions. With Turner, this knowledge is intuitive. He does not much believe in market research. This is the case with almost all creative business geniuses—they know what the public wants. The rest of us, however, have to do our *learning* in order to know what the public wants.

> **LESSON #3:** Creative business geniuses often take huge risks—or what appear to others to be huge risks.

Because they have faith in their knowledge of what the public wants and faith in their ability to add value, creative business geniuses can take huge risks in buying assets. Turner's associates said it was a bad idea to buy a UHF station. Turner bought it anyway, because he believed he could quickly add value. Over and over again in his career, Turner took risks that would leave the rest of us shaking in our shoes. He was fearless, but fearless for a reason.

On December 27, 1976, Turner read an article in *Broadcasting* magazine that HBO had gone on RCA's new SATCOM II communications satellite. SATCOM II was an antenna in space. Signals went up to the satellite and were rebroadcast back to receivers on Earth. Before this, the use of satellites for television did not exist.

Ted Turner was one of the first to visualize what this meant for television (cable television in particular). Cable had been, up to this point, primarily a way for areas outside urban centers (where the television stations existed) to receive clear TV signals.

Cable systems had erected a series of microwave towers on high points that relayed signals "hill to hill" until they came to one of the cable company's towns. In the town, the cable company connected the individual homes to a line from the microwave tower. Satellite transmission meant you did not need the microwave towers anymore.

To Turner, satellite also meant that he could dramatically increase the reach of WTCG, gain thousands of additional viewers beyond the Atlanta market, and, with the larger audience, dramatically increase his advertising revenues. This was revolutionary thinking. HBO planned to make its money by charging individual subscribers for its channel. Turner would give WTCG (renamed "The Superstation") to cable companies free of charge and make his money on ad revenue. Once again, he saw the future and acted on his vision.

This was, to put it mildly, a gutsy move. At the time, very few cable systems owned the equipment that could receive the signals sent back down to Earth from the satellite. And there were very few uplinks in existence to send the signals up—the ones that did exist cost $750,000 (real money back then). A long-term lease on the satellite cost millions. And no one was really sure if what Turner planned to do was exactly legal.

What he planned to do was send Atlanta Braves' and Atlanta Hawks' games (both teams he now owned) and *The Flintstones, Mr. Ed, The Munsters,* and movies licensed from Hollywood to wherever in the country a cable system had a satellite receiver and agreed to put his station on the air.

And out there in TV land, they loved Turner's station, just as they had in Atlanta. The Superstation, along with HBO, helped fuel cable's growth and its move into the urban centers. Cable was no longer just a way for remote outposts to receive clear television signals. With The Superstation and HBO, it was a way of getting more content than the three networks provided.

Ted Turner had reinvented TV and taken a lot of people by surprise. And lots of people were mad. Professional sports were mad because he was broadcasting games in other teams' territories. Hollywood was mad because he was paying to show movies and series reruns in the Atlanta market but beaming them across the country. The networks were mad because he was moving in on national ad revenue.

Ted Turner saw the future and knew professional sports, Hollywood, and the networks would come after him (which they did). So to hedge his bets, before The Superstation was even up on the satellite, he was mapping out plans for the first twenty-four-hour all-news television network—CNN. Talk about vision!

LESSON #4: Always look for the next big idea.

Creative business geniuses are always looking for the next big idea that will drive the business. They know that without new ideas the business will stagnate and eventually die.

CNN changed the world. It brought unfolding events live to the living rooms of America. Presidents and dictators became addicted to it.

This was, again, a huge risk. None of the big media players—companies with ten and twenty times Turner's assets—wanted to touch twenty-four-hour news. It had never been done before. Nobody knew what the audience would be or how much advertising revenue was possible. Or how much it would cost to build and maintain. By personally guaranteeing the money to build CNN, Turner could have lost everything.

How Turner even decided to build a twenty-four-hour news network is something of a mystery. He had long said he wanted nothing to do with the news—it was depressing. Whatever prompted him to come up with the idea, Turner was pushed into doing it. He had acquired rights to the last spot on RCA's satellite SATCOM III and he had to declare he was going to use the spot or lose his space. He declared he would use the slot for CNN.

Although Ted Turner has had his setbacks through the years, he has shown himself time after time as a creative genius and simply one of the best there is at buying and building businesses. He is so good because he:

- Sees the future
- Knows what the public wants
- Takes huge risks based on his ability to add value
- Is always looking for the next big idea

RUPERT MURDOCH

While Ted Turner has, at least for the time being, exited the media stage, resigning his post as vice-chairman of AOL Time-Warner, Rupert Murdoch is still very much involved. As chairman and CEO of News Corporation, Murdoch presides over a global empire of newspapers, TV networks, magazines, and movies, an empire that he built from the ground up. His worth in 2005 was $6.7 billion, according to *Forbes* magazine. His media properties reach two-thirds of the people in the world.

Rupert Murdoch has been called bad things. For a man who owns so much media, he gets a lot of bad press. This owes much to his ownership of sensationalist tabloids like the *Sun* in England and the *New York Post* in America; Fox network reality hits like *Cops, America's Most Wanted,* A *Current Affair,* and *American Idol;* and the conservative, for some, FOX News.

The knock against Murdoch (other than the concern he is trying to take over the media world) is that he is lowering cultural standards, appealing to the "lowest common denominator," and debasing civilization.

While Murdoch does own the *Sun*—home to the Page 3 Girl (topless beauties appearing on page three of the paper)—and a network that showed *Joe Millionaire,* he also owns the *Times* of London, one of the most prestigious newspapers in the world, and the National Geographic Channel.

Murdoch's FOX network is responsible for critically acclaimed series like *Ally McBeal, American Family, 24,* and *The Simpsons,* considered by some to be the greatest show ever to appear on television. His studio—20th Century Fox—has brought out movies like *Cast Away* with Tom Hanks, the animated *Ice Age,* and *Waiting to Exhale.*

Murdoch, like Turner:

- Sees the future
- Knows what the public wants
- Has time and again taken huge risks to buy assets because he believes he can add value
- And Murdoch has, throughout his career, chased the big idea (the REALLY, REALLY, REALLY BIG IDEA)

What differentiates Murdoch and Turner is the scope of their visions. Turner's vision is based on cable and, primarily, the United States (although CNN is more than an American network).

Murdoch's vision is global and encompasses most forms of media—newspapers, books, magazines, cable programming, ownership of television stations, movies, satellite TV.

Murdoch was born in Australia (he became an American citizen in 1985) and graduated from Oxford. Like Turner, he took over the family business (daily and Sunday newspapers in Adelaide, Australia) at a young age and quickly put it in order. That accomplished, he set out on a media-buying spree that has been going on now for fifty years.

A few other media conglomerates are larger than Murdoch's company (News Corporation), but none has the international reach, none was built by a single individual to the degree NewsCorp was, and none is so closely held (the Murdoch family owns over 30 percent). No big media company is as much a reflection of one man's vision. Only Turner Broadcasting/Ted Turner and Viacom/Sumner Redstone come close.

Rupert Murdoch has had and executed so many big ideas that it is difficult to choose just a couple. Three famous ones are his reinvention of the *Sun* newspaper in London, the creation (along with Barry Diller) of FOX Broadcasting—the fourth network that most thought was impossible—and the launch of FOX News.

In creating and developing the *Sun,* FOX Broadcasting, and FOX News, Murdoch had one Big Idea. He expressed that Big Idea as "anybody who, within the law of the land, provides a service which the public wants at a price it can afford is providing a public service."

> Murdoch's idea was: standards be damned—give people what they want to buy.

Enlightened marketing gurus have been telling us this forever. But there is resistance in the media world—in media, responsible companies are supposed to "uphold standards."

Murdoch bought the *Sun* in 1969. It was a failing broadsheet with a circulation of 850,000. He transformed it into a tabloid and gave the readers more pictures, more TV and radio information, more gossip, more stories about the royals, more local news, shorter, easier-to-read stories, much more sports, more sex, more sensationalism, and the famous Page 3 girls.

By the end of 1970, the *Sun* had circulation of 1.7 million—an incredible doubling of the number of readers in a little more than a year. The *Sun* became the largest English-language newspaper in the world. Revenue from the *Sun* (and another sex-and-scandal paper in Britain—*News of the World*) fueled Murdoch's worldwide expansion for years to come.

Like Ted Turner's game on UHF TV, Murdoch had taken a losing property and quickly turned it around by giving people what they wanted (adding value)—although there were some who did not like what the people wanted and disliked the fact that Murdoch gave it to them.

FOX Broadcasting, the fourth network, came about as the result of two acquisitions—20th Century Fox and a group of independent television stations. The purchase of both properties, at roughly the same time, was a huge financial risk and could have easily taken down News Corporation if things had not worked out. And many believed that starting a fourth network was a foolhardy enterprise.

> Creative business geniuses know what the public wants.

Murdoch and Barry Diller (whom Murdoch hired to run the network) believed they could succeed because they felt the major networks were not giving people what they wanted. There was a safe, middle-of-the-road sameness to network programming that was out of touch with America. They found where the networks were failing and pushed the edge of the envelope.

After some misses, *The Simpsons* debuted on FOX and Bart Simpson accomplished the impossible—he almost single handedly created a fourth national network. If network programming was the 1950s' *Father Knows Best,* this was not it.

Homer Simpson worked at the local nuclear plant, just down the street from the toxic waste dump and prison. His family was unhappy, cynical, and alienated. Bart was an "Underachiever—and Proud of It."

The Simpsons pushed FOX television to the top of the Neilson ratings, just three years after the network had come on air. Then came *Married…with Children*—the story of Al and Peg Bundy and their kids and a dog named Buck. The Bundys sniped at each other, bickered, and belched. Peg was the worst wife, cook, and mother on the planet. Al was an inadequate provider, lover, and father.

Then came *A Current Affair.* It was to *60 Minutes* what the *New York Post* was to the *New York Times.* The show covered wet T-shirt contests, hooker heroine addicts, and cheating wives. Maury Povich, the host of the show, has said that what really differentiated *A Current Affair* from other TV news programs was that it never tried to be fair. The *New York Times* said of *A Current Affair*, "Nothing short of vile. What kind of people do we want to be?"

As a final example of Murdoch's creative genius, consider FOX News. Launched in 1996, FOX News has succeeded in doing something few thought possible—it has, as of the first part of 2003, replaced CNN as the top twenty-four-hour news channel in America. FOX News' success rests, again, on Murdoch's belief that you should give the public what it wants.

FOX News debuted in 1996. Murdoch entered the news market at a time when all-news channels, including CNN, were suffering. Audiences generally were declining. CNN's prime-time viewing numbers within the U.S. rarely exceeded one million. It was being squeezed by cable newcomers like Lifetime and Discovery.

Murdoch believed there was an opportunity to challenge CNN and to increase viewership by offering more conservative content—which FOX News provides. As he said at the launch, for FOX News to compete with CNN, "We may have to develop another expert source on Cuba other than CNN's bureau chief, Fidel Castro." This referred to Ted Turner's trips to Cuba to visit Castro, who was an avid CNN viewer. (Part of Murdoch's dislike of Turner was the latter's "liberalism." Part of Turner's dislike of Murdoch was the fact he came after CNN with FOX News.)

To get FOX News launched as widely as possible, Murdoch decided to offer large cash incentives to cable operators. Usually, cable operators pay a fee per subscriber to channels. Murdoch, by contrast, elected to pay the cable operators large fees for every subscriber they brought to FOX News. This was a phenomenal change to the economics of the whole industry.

As of this writing, FOX News has blown past CNN. Some may disagree with the conservative bent of FOX News, but there is, unquestionably, an audience for a twenty-four-hour news channel with attitude, one that takes a position (compared to CNN which, for the most part, presents the news "raw").

Ted Turner and Rupert Murdoch—two creative geniuses, with a rare knack for big ideas. We can't all be Turners and Murdochs, but we can pick up a tip or two about developing ideas from these masters. Taking a page from these idea giants, here are four things you can do to improve your ability to create your own lightning in a bottle:

- Keep your **eye on the future.**
- Do everything you can to **understand what the public wants.**
- Don't be afraid to **take risks** based on prudent analysis.
- **Keep your radar on for big ideas.**

What else can you do to improve your new-product success rate? Beyond taking a page from the idea masters, most everyone would benefit from following a better new-product process. Our new-product process is called Idea Engineering, and the next chapter includes everything you need to know to master this powerful new tool.

CHAPTER 11

IDEA ENGINEERING: SEVEN STEPS

So far, you've read about how American business develops ideas, pitfalls with common new-product techniques like focus groups and market segmentation, what can be learned from creative idea geniuses, and what new product success looks like. You've learned that nine out of ten new products fail. The objective was to present the lay of the land—the way that new products are developed today. A lot of what has been covered is how *not* to develop new products. At this point you may be feeling like there must be a better way. There is, and it starts right now.

We now turn from the status quo to something new and revolutionary. Idea Engineering is a simple process that allows for dramatic improvement in developing new products. It is based on decades of new-product development work, and has been used successfully across a wide range of new products, from ironing boards to satellite radio.

If you have been slumping in your chair and getting comfortable, now is the time to do like your mother said—sit up straight and pay attention!

This chapter describes a repeatable, seven-step system for developing new ideas to drive your business. We call it Idea Engineering, and it's the surest way we know to capture lightning in a bottle.

You can call it Idea Engineering or anything you want. And you can use it anytime you want. It is a simple, straightforward process and not at all mysterious. You need some creativity, but, more than that, you need to apply lots of time and elbow grease to the system in order to develop ideas. With time, practice, and experience you will be amazed with the results. You will be able to create your own lightning in a bottle—HUGE IDEAS—while others stumble.

> There are creative people in this world—idea people, people who change the world with great intuitive leaps.

Albert Einstein comes to mind, William Shakespeare, Picasso. On a more commercial level, people like Ted Turner and Rupert Murdoch, discussed in the previous chapter.

> These people are not you (most of you).

They are something special, and how they come up with ideas, how their minds work, is, to some degree, unfathomable. How they come up with their ideas is their way.

For the rest of us, there is Idea Engineering.

Processes and systems can be boring and tedious. So we move through this chapter at a fast pace. Here is the cookbook for creating powerful new products and services.

SEVEN STEPS: IDEA ENGINEERING

1. Learn
2. Develop Working Theories
3. Develop Ideas and Concepts from the Working Theories
4. Conduct Financial Due Diligence
5. Talk to Consumers: Not in Groups, But One Person at a Time
6. Iterate the Concepts by Listening to Consumers
7. Take the Best Concepts Coming Out of the Interviews and "Monetize" Them: Predict Real-World Revenue

STEP #1: LEARN

"Learn" refers to reading all the important information ever published on the topic at hand.

This sounds simple. But this step is rarely done in a comprehensive fashion. Why? One, it takes time, lots of time. Everything important ever published on a topic can run to thousands of pages. Two, people fall into the trap of thinking they know everything important about the topic at hand, or at least enough. The fact is that you can always pick up new and critical information by a review of the literature. Reading about the topic builds the foundation for coming up with ideas.

This is a step than can save you a lot of heartache. Many of the mistakes companies will make in the future have already been made by other companies in the past (and sometimes by the same company).

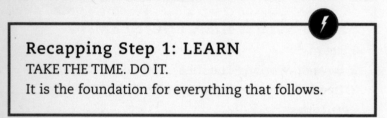

Recapping Step 1: LEARN
TAKE THE TIME. DO IT.
It is the foundation for everything that follows.

STEP #2: DEVELOP WORKING THEORIES

You have done your learning by reading everything important ever written on the topic. Now it is time to develop "working theories" from that learning. Let's take a look at what we mean by working theories.

Working theories are:

- Your beliefs, which you write down, about what the consumer thinks or does not think
- What the consumer wants or does not want when it comes to the topic
- What has worked, or not worked, in the past and why
- How another industry solved a similar problem to the one you are facing

Working theories are the foundation for the new ideas (or concepts) that you create in the next step. We normally develop ten to twenty different working theories. Below is an example of one single working theory from an actual project we worked on.

Business Issue:

- How do you create "fun" in a retail environment?
- Underlying belief: Fun can be used in a retail environment as a competitive weapon, and to differentiate the experience.
- What should you consider before you try to build fun into your retail experience?

Example of a Working Theory:

- Working Theory: CONSUMERS GET BORED QUICKLY.
- Whatever you do to make retail fun and entertain folks, you have to change it pretty often.
- Otherwise consumers will think of you not as fun, but as boring.

This working theory comes from studying an extremely long and complicated textbook full of very big words which was part of what we studied in our first step (Learning). The book's title is *Well-Being: The Foundations of Hedonic Psychology.* It's one of the few books written that has any science about the emotion called "fun." Among many other things, the book talks about:

The hedonic treadmill. People adapt to improving circumstances to the point of affective neutrality. An experience that is routine and fully expected becomes affectively neutral.

Which means, in normal language, consumers get bored quickly. Maybe we have long suspected that, but the textbook provides a scientific basis for the concept.

So based on our learning that consumers get bored quickly, there is a fact-based foundation that can be used to develop working theories.

Here's how this working theory guided us in developing ideas for a fun retail environment.

- Consumers want a new experience on a regular basis.
- That is why Warner Brothers stores, Planet Hollywood, or Rainforest Café (and we could go on and on), failed. They did not refresh the offering.
- They sank too much capital into the original build-out and did not have enough money to refresh or change it.
- LESSON: Fun stuff in a retail environment should be inexpensive so it can be constantly refreshed.

So later when we are coming up with ideas and writing concepts, let's make sure that we do not include ideas that require a lot of build-out capital. The consumer is going to get bored soon with what we built and we won't have any money left to refresh.

Just by doing the first two steps—learning and writing the working theories—you are already *way* ahead in the new-idea ballgame and on your way to creating ideas that will work. Why?

- You have spent probably one hundred to one hundred fifty hours doing nuts and bolts preparation.
- You are building a foundation before you start creating new ideas.

- Spending this time is critical.
- Hardly anybody does it in a systematic way.

Creating new ideas that work has more to do with solid, systematic preparation—learning and then writing working theories—than it does with on-the-spot inspiration and creativity.

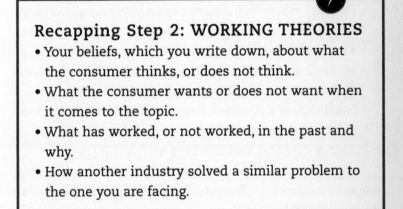

Recapping Step 2: WORKING THEORIES

- Your beliefs, which you write down, about what the consumer thinks, or does not think.
- What the consumer wants or does not want when it comes to the topic.
- What has worked, or not worked, in the past and why.
- How another industry solved a similar problem to the one you are facing.

STEP #3: DEVELOP IDEAS AND CONCEPTS

Here is where the rubber meets the road, because now it's time to come up with the ideas. But don't freak out: you don't have to find the final solution in this step. You only have to get started. In fact, you can be completely wrong with your ideas at this point and still come out a big winner using the seven-step process.

Let's do an example—we'll switch from fun in a retail environment to, believe it or not, selling buffalo meat.

THE PROBLEM: Not enough people are buying buffalo meat. Supply among the ranchers who raise buffalo is outpacing the limited demand that exists. Prices are dropping.

STEP #1 LEARNING

You secure and study everything important known about buffalo (and there is not much).

STEP #2 WORKING THEORIES

You write some working theories. Here are a few.

- Awareness of buffalo-meat products is low
- Perceptions may be negative
- Perception that buffalo are extinct or endangered (why haven't I seen it on a menu before?)
- Perception that meat is gamey or tough
- Must first deal with existing "negatives" before consumers would consider any "positives"
- Need to find a positive hook that would encourage people to try buffalo

STEP #3 DEVELOPING THE CONCEPTS

Based on your learning and working theories, you write a bunch of concepts. In this case, the end job is to deliver language that the buffalo industry can use in advertising and public relations to get people to buy more buffalo. Here are some examples of concepts.

EXAMPLES OF IDEAS AND CONCEPTS

Buffalo. A delicacy as wonderful as where it comes from.

Imagine a meadow high in the Rocky Mountains. Green grass, mountain wildflowers. Snow-capped

---

peaks in the distance. An Alpine stream. Here the buffalo live wild. Try this delicacy that is as marvelous as the place it lives.

Buffalo. Raised in the Great West.

From the plateaus of New Mexico, through the mountains of Colorado, to the Wyoming frontier. Buffalo—authentic Western cuisine. USDA inspected and approved.

Before there was Beef, there was Buffalo.

Native Americans knew it hundreds of years ago. Westerners know it today. Buffalo is the original American meat. Now with large, ranch-raised herds in all fifty states, it's your turn. USDA inspected and approved.

What can run thirty mph, jump a six-foot fence, and survive temperatures forty-five degrees below zero?

Buffalo—long enjoyed in the West for its great taste. You are what you eat. USDA inspected and approved.

Later, you take these concepts to consumers—interviewing them one at a time—and you find…*they are all wrong, off track, and won't sell more buffalo.*

The important thing is *not* that you were wrong about the language you showed consumers to get them to buy more buffalo. The purpose of the ideas and concepts you showed was to get consumers thinking, and get them talking about how they feel about buffalo meat. This is a critical point. In more traditional market research, you would be dead if you got to this point and did not have winning language. In our process it makes no difference—other steps that follow will provide the critical answers and language that will sell more buffalo meat.

It turns out many of the working theories are wrong and, hence, the concepts are wrong. Consumers don't care where a buffalo is raised, how fast it can run, or whether or not Native Americans ate it. By listening to consumers react to the words we show them, it turns out they want to know:

- Does it taste good?
- Is it tender?
- Is it good for you?

Early on, by listening to consumers react, you discover your mistakes and write new concepts. In the end, you have a new tag line, and new language and positioning that captures the consumer's attention:

BUFFALO—TENDER, TASTY, AND HEALTHY

Many who have tried it like it better than beef. It's tender, flavorful, and something different.

And although it has the great taste of beef, buffalo is *lower* in fat and cholesterol and *higher* in protein and nutrients than beef, chicken, turkey, or pork.

And the new concept and tag line work. Consumers like them, they want to try buffalo based on these simple positionings, and all is good. The client was the National Bison Association. Ted Turner, the biggest buffalo rancher in the U.S., sat in on our presentation about what we learned, and complimented us afterwards. Turner's newest venture? Opening a chain of national restaurants featuring buffalo— Ted's Montana Grill.

Recapping Step 3: DEVELOP IDEAS AND CONCEPTS

- Ideas are based on earlier steps, LEARNING and the WORKING THEORIES.
- Your ideas and concepts do not come out of a vacuum.
- It really makes no difference at this point if your ideas or good or bad. Steps that follow will sort that out.

STEP #4: FINANCIAL DUE DILIGENCE

This is simple, but it is often not done until time and money have been wasted. It means that after you come up with the ideas, take some time and project whether they are financially sound.

Financial analysis at this point can be simple back-of-the-envelope math. It does not have to be intricate and involve dozens of spreadsheets. Make your assumptions, do basic financials, and see if the idea is in the ballpark.

Do not omit this step because you think it will be too involved or time consuming. It is a waste of everyone's time to come up with ideas that will never work financially.

With truly big ideas, it rarely takes sophisticated analysis to figure out it is a big thing. Big ideas usually pencil out very easily. In fact, if it takes reams of paper and complicated analysis to prove an idea will make money, be on guard.

Recapping Step 4: FINANCIAL ANALYSIS
- Determine if your idea is financially sound.
- It's not necessary to create a detailed analysis, so don't get bogged down.
- Do enough to know if your idea is in the ballpark of penciling out financially.

STEP #5: TALK TO CONSUMERS, NOT IN GROUPS, BUT ONE PERSON AT A TIME

Remember the buffalo example? If buffalo had been handled with focus groups, chances are the problem would have not been solved. One or more of those losing concepts—the wrong answer—would have gone forward.

When it comes to developing new ideas—and this is absolutely critical—don't use focus groups. *Interview people one person at a time.*

This probably goes contrary to everything you have ever heard. In fact, hardly anybody every talks about one-on-one, in-depth interviews. The main reason is that interviewing people one at time takes a lot of time. Lots and lots of time. We usually interview thirty to thirty-five individuals, spending an hour with each.

Here's what likely would have happened if the buffalo research had been conducted using focus groups. Everybody is in a hurry (including the focus-group moderator, who wants to make as much money as possible in the least amount of time possible), so all three focus groups are scheduled in a single day.

It's all over in an afternoon and a night. At the end of the night you are trying to figure out what the people said and what they meant because:

- It all happened too fast.
- During the seven hours you did not have time to think about and come to conclusions about what people were saying.
- You have *not* iterated, improved, and rewritten your ideas and concepts.
- You're only beginning to realize that something was wrong with the ideas you presented.

So what you might do, not wanting to take the time and/or spend the money on another round of focus groups, is take the best concept out of the ones you presented—and you're wrong. And it doesn't work. And somebody takes the fall.

In the one-on-one interviews, at the seven-hour mark you've finished one day of interviewing—you have listened to seven people. You've got twenty-three more people to go, another twenty-three hours.

But you know at the end of seven hours that something is wrong because:

- The pace is far more leisurely than focus groups—one person talking at a time, not eight at the same time—you're able to analyze and figure out what that is.
- You write ideas that will work.
- The next day you show your new ideas to the next set of respondents.
- The ideas get stronger and better.

One-on-one, in-depth interviews are much more effective for developing successful ideas than focus groups. Here is a key reason that interviews work so much better in developing new products and services: they take a long time to do.

- They take long enough and you hear the same things often enough that only a complete idiot could miss the message.
- With one-on-one interviews, the meaning of what has been said is never a mystery.
- Consumers' reactions to your ideas are never open to multiple, conflicting interpretations.

This is not spending extra time for the sake of spending extra time. This is absolutely necessary if you want success with new ideas.

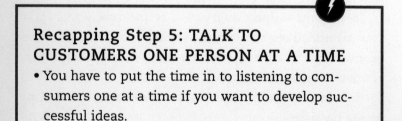

Recapping Step 5: TALK TO CUSTOMERS ONE PERSON AT A TIME
- You have to put the time in to listening to consumers one at a time if you want to develop successful ideas.

> • Do this one thing and you will immediately increase your odds of developing better ideas.

STEP #6: ITERATE THE CONCEPTS BY TALKING TO CONSUMERS

You already know what this one is. It means you revise and improve your ideas as you get feedback from the eventual users—or, as in the case of buffalo, you throw out *every* idea you had and start from scratch.

Iterating takes time. You can't iterate successfully between two focus groups. As you listen carefully to consumers—one at a time—you will hear the things that need to be changed in your ideas. Some of these things are simple language changes and some are alterations to the core idea and some take you in new directions.

Never go into interviews with consumers thinking you have the final answer.

Always be ready to scramble.

Scrambling—adjusting your ideas as you learn—is another way to immediately improve your ideas.

Recapping Step 6: ITERATE IDEAS WHILE TALKING TO CONSUMERS

- Listen carefully to what consumers say.
- Modify your product or service, or how you talk about your product, based on careful listening.
- Sometimes just changing a word or two can make a big difference in consumers' interest.

> • This is completely different than traditional mar-
> ket research beliefs, where you must hold ideas
> constant. Don't follow the masses here—they are
> wrong.

STEP #7: TAKE THE BEST CONCEPTS COMING OUT OF THE INTERVIEWS AND MONETIZE THEM: PREDICT REAL-WORLD REVENUE

You've put in your time–you've done your learning, you've written your working theories, you have developed and written your ideas, you have sat through the interviews and iterated your ideas. All told, you're 175 plus hours into this, just counting the six steps we've talked about and not counting any internal meetings on the subject. There is no reason you can't do this yourself, other than the intense time commitment.

You think you have something. Now it's time to find out how much your ideas are worth—in cold, hard cash, in incremental dollar volume to the company. None of the time spent thus far means anything if your idea is not going to drive revenue.

How do you predict revenue?

With a quantitative consumer survey, typically interviewing eight hundred to one thousand people who may be interested in your product.

Do *not* do a survey that just gives you "market research" gibberish like "18 percent said they would be 'very likely' to walk a mile for a Camel. Another 23 percent said they would be 'somewhat likely' to walk a mile for a Camel."

What you need is, "Idea X will generate $502 million in incremental revenue the first twelve months and $1.33 billion in the second twelve months."

Monetizing ideas is the most technical of the seven steps, as it typically involves surveying one thousand consumers by telephone or over the Internet. Special expertise is helpful in designing the questionnaire used to collect data, the method in which people are screened to participate, and other matters. Some, but not most, companies have the expertise on staff to do this kind of work.

When attempting to monetize, these points are key:

- It is best left to experts with new-product/idea-development experience.
- Survey data tends to overestimate potential, so the raw data has to be discounted from what consumers claim they will do.
- It takes experience to produce accurate projections.

If you choose to do it yourself, the basic exercise is to describe the new product or service in one to three short paragraphs, then ask consumers if they intend to buy the product or not. More specifically, you ask the likelihood that they will buy the new product/service. Because consumers overstate reality in surveys, it is necessary to reduce what consumers say they will buy in order to get a more accurate estimate of true demand.

Recapping Step 7: TAKE THE BEST CONCEPTS COMING OUT OF THE INTERVIEWS AND MONETIZE THEM: PREDICT REAL-WORLD REVENUE

- Use large-scale consumer survey research to predict real-world revenue.
- It is a technical process best left to people with expertise in consumer research.

THERE YOU HAVE IT: SEVEN STEPS

It works, over and over again. It is the recipe for creating your own lightning in a bottle, whenever you need a big idea.

Part of the reason the process works is because it provides a system for doing something that is hard to do. It is a time-tested, repeatable way to develop big ideas.

- You're not trying to pull new ideas out of the hat.
- You're moving step-by-step to a solution.
- You're building a foundation, then you're trying to make sense of that foundation with working theories.
- You're coming up with ideas based on working theories.
- You're getting feedback from the consumer.

And the system is self-correcting; if you are off track, it is almost impossible to move forward because it is plainly obvious that you are off track.

Part of the reason the seven steps work is the amount of time and focus they take. This is a time-consuming way of going about things. To come up with ideas that are successful in the market, you have to spend time at it. It's not magic—it's just a system that works. It will create lightning in a bottle for you—over and over again.

The Idea Engineering process described in this chapter has yet to fail us, and if you follow the discipline, it *will* work for you, too!

The following chapter illustrates how Idea Engineering works, step-by-step. The example used is that you are given the job of coming up with a new record label. Not an easy job given the intense change in the music industry—iPods, shrinking CD sales, and increasing downloading of music. The music industry is in chaos, so it's not an easy category in which to create miracles. But armed with a sound system and a process, you have a much, much better chance of success.

CHAPTER 12

IDEA ENGINEERING: LET'S START A RECORD LABEL

We looked at the seven Idea Engineering steps in the last chapter. Now let's look at the seven steps in a little more detail, so when you need to use them, you have a better idea how to do so. The easiest way to understand the process is with a detailed, step-by-step example, so we're going to create a new record label using the Idea Engineering process.

SEVEN STEPS: IDEA ENGINEERING
1. Learn
2. Develop Working Theories
3. Develop Ideas and Concepts from the Working Theories
4. Conduct Financial Due Diligence

5. Talk to Consumers One at a Time
6. Iterate the Concepts by Listening to Consumers
7. Take the Best Concepts Coming out of the Interviews and Monetize Them

Let's say you're a marketing consultant, and a billionaire calls you up. He's a real billionaire, maybe the fifth richest guy in the world. He made his money in software, but he is not in that anymore. He's freelance now, looking for opportunities, looking to move up from the fifth spot. And he is looking to have some fun, because, well, now that he is the fifth richest guy in the world, it is not all about money anymore.

The billionaire—let's call him Bill—calls you up (let's call you Andy). Bill says, "Andy, heard you are a great idea guy, came up with the idea for a new disposable Styrofoam cup, fabulous concept—the convenience of Styrofoam but biodegradable—fantastic."

And you say, "Thanks, Bill, that's quite a compliment coming from you, the fifth richest man in the world."

And Bill says, "I've got an assignment for you, Andy."

And you say, "Terrific. What is it?"

And Bill says, "I'm thinking of getting into the music business. I want you to tell me how I should do it."

After you think for a second, you say, "I don't know much about the music business, Bill, but let me understand. Are we talking about the rat-hole music business where the kids are stealing music off the Internet so sales are falling like a rock…that music business?"

Bill says, "Yes, that very one. Sure, the music business has problems, but, you know, I love music. I want to be a big part of the music business. And I want to make lots of money doing it, because I don't do anything that doesn't make lots of money."

Bill says, "You do your thing, Andy. Seven steps, right? I skimmed your book...well, actually, my assistant skimmed your book and wrote me a summary on a Post-It note. I'll pay you a million dollars. How's that sound?"

And before you can say, boy, I could use a million dollars, Bill says, "I need the answer in three months, okay?" And, before you can say, okay, Bill says, "I'm putting your check for a million dollars in the mail, don't disappoint me." And he hangs up.

Your Assignment: Figure out how Bill becomes a big part of the music business and how he makes lots of money doing that.

First thing: are you afraid? Considering you know almost nothing about the music business and that what you do know about the music business is not hopeful, you would have to be nuts to want to get into the music business right now.

Are you afraid you won't be able to come up with an answer? NO. You're not afraid for three reasons.

#1. You have a system that works—seven steps that time after time come up with the right answer.

#2. It does not matter that you do not know anything about the music business. What you have is fresh perspective (look at the mess the guys who know the music business have gotten it into). And soon you will have conducted your due diligence and learned much about how the business has developed. The system will take it from there.

This may be hard to believe. But, honestly, it really does not matter how much you know about an industry or a business before you get started. If you use Idea Engineering, the system works.

#3. Sure, the assignment is difficult, but there is opportunity in turmoil. If it were easy, everybody would be doing it.

Let's take the scenario through the seven steps.

STEP #1: LEARNING

First, we have to do our learning. But before we can do the learning somebody has to assemble the materials to learn from. So you call our guy that assembles everything important ever written about the music business—let's call him Tommy.

You have to have a Tommy—he's the one who gives you the materials to start building your foundation. Tommy has to have many good qualities—he has to be a whiz at gathering information on the Internet, and he has to be fast, because your clients are always in a hurry. He has to be a quick study, because you never have time to give him a two-hour briefing and, most importantly, he has to have the ability to sift the grain from the chaff.

Remember, you're going to read everything *important* ever written about the music industry. That does not mean everything written about the music business. It means the important stuff.

> Usually, at least 50 percent of the things written about anything are *unimportant* or just plain wrong. Tommy has to have a sense of what is important and what is not.

Tommy goes to work. A week later he delivers the material. It's five hundred pages, organized by topic. It covers how the music business works, who the key players are, how the contracts are done, who makes the money, trends for the last twenty years, what the artists think of the labels, what the labels think of the artists, what the record buyers think of the labels, what the record buyers think of music in the last several years, Napster, Aimster, and so on.

The material is not unlike the kind of stuff you gather if you are considering an acquisition or want to learn about a competitor. But here, the use is different. Here, you are feeding your marketing/idea brain.

This is raw material—data from the Recording Industry of America, excerpts from monographs, trade magazine articles, and the like. With it you start building. You read through it once. You see what connections your brain makes with the stuff Tommy pulled. Then you read it a second time. Sometimes you need Tommy to do more hunting because what he pulled does not answer all your questions.

You're almost two weeks into it now—a week for Tommy to pull information, plus five days of reading and thinking. You now have a whole list of things you've learned about the music business. Here are a few of them:

- It was good, then it was bad, and then it turned ugly.
- In the 1990s, CD shipments increased, on average, 15 percent a year.
- In 2000, the year Napster came on the scene, the growth stopped dead in its tracks.
- 2001 was down 4 percent.
- 2002 was down 9 percent.
- By late 2003 the industry is reporting that 30 percent of CD sales have vanished in the past three years—ouch and ouch again.
- As of early 2005, there are some signs of life for music sales—driven largely by new distribution and consumption schemes such as the $1 per song download, Apple's iPod, and the like.

Part of the decline is continued stealing—the recording industry killed the original anything-goes Napster with lawsuits, but a host of harder-to-kill offshoots took Napster's place. More people download music now than in Napster's heyday.

But the decline is not entirely due to stealing music on the Internet. Other things within the music industry look like they are contributing. The consolidation in the industry may have something to do with it. The Telecom Act of 1995 removed restrictions on the number of radio stations a company could own in a single market. The result has been the development of huge radio conglomerates, companies that own thousands of radio stations and control entire markets.

Big companies inevitably require standardization, so programming choices are being taken out of the hands of the local stations. Programs at corporate headquarters are dictating what the local stations play. Increasingly, the radio stations sound the same.

Everybody is at everybody else's throat. Artists are trashing fans because they are stealing music. The labels are suing everyone, including thirteen-year-old kids, in an attempt to put the genie back in the bottle. The artists are saying the labels are cheating them (nothing new). The music fans are saying the labels are a bunch of criminals who gouge the fans and cheat the artists.

Man, it's a mess and it looks like it is going to take a long time for the industry to climb back to the lofty levels it once enjoyed.

STEP #2: WORKING THEORIES

So you have the learning. Now it's time to start on the working theories. This is the beginning of the creative process. It is taking raw material and seeing what connections you can make.

When developing working theories, it is best to have a partner to help. You can be creative by yourself, but two is often better than one (*but* more than two or three is probably not going to be productive—see chapter 8, "Less Is More").

Here are a few of the working theories you come up with:

#1. The learning clearly says that in this industry, there are big, bad villains. The villains are the labels and the radio station conglomerates.

Working theory #2 is a connection you make with #1: if there are villains, there may be opportunities to be the hero—the guy in shining armor who rides in on the white horse and saves the girl.

Working theory #3 is pure conjecture: it may be complete hogwash, but it does not have to be true at this stage of the game. You just need something to start with. So working theory #3 says "Free" (as in stealing music over the Internet) is a tough proposition with which to compete. But maybe the people getting music for free on the Internet might be willing to pay at least something for what they otherwise get for free. They have no qualms about taking it for free because they see much of the money they pay for music going to the villains—the labels—and little of it going to the artists. *But what if more of the money went to the artists instead of the labels (the villains)?*

These working theories are contrary to many of the hypotheses you saw in literature during the learning phase. One of the popular ideas in the literature was that labels should band together and create their own Napster—one for which consumers would pay a monthly subscription.

Their idea is that the labels open their catalogs to a third-party digital music service provider who aggregates the multiple catalogs and makes them available to consumers on the Internet—pay $10 a month and be able to download fifteen songs.

Those promoting this idea think it will work because they think consumers who now download songs for free will be willing to pay if they get features like better quality music files and virus protection.

This makes no sense to you because your learning and resulting working theory says a major reason consumers have no qualms about stealing music is that they think too much of the money goes to the villains.

But it is an idea—one that you should include as a straw concept against your own concepts.

STEP #3: DEVELOP YOUR IDEAS: WRITE CONCEPTS

We have our learning. We have some working theories. It's time to weave this together into actionable ideas that will make Bill (the billionaire) lots of money and a major player in the music industry.

So here is an idea that comes out of the learning and the working theories:

- Be a hero by starting a cooperative that give new artists with good music the chance to record their music.
- This is not a label. It is an anti-label. Every artist in the cooperative owns a piece of it.
- The message to the fans is that this is an artists' organization, not a label that takes all the money. You are going to want to pay for this music. You are going to want to pay a fair price, say $7 for the CD, not the $18 the label charges so they can ride around in the limos. You will want to pay because the money goes to the artists, and that means the

artists, whose music you like, will continue to make music.

- And, anyway, *this is not about money, it's about music.*

Those are the ideas. Now you tighten them up into messages that you can present and get reaction to in research. Something like this:

THE GOOD GUYS' HONEST, TRUEBLUE MUSIC CO-OP (G2H-TMC)

At G2H-TMC, it's not about money, it's about music. A collaborative music cooperative, owned by the artists, not the conglomerates.

Created to bring great, distinctive music to you, the music lover.

Created to give the artists, finally, what they are worth and deserve.

Created to give you music for a value. We've taken the middleman conglomerates out of the equation, which means we can sell the music for a lot less—and the money goes to the artists, not the conglomerates.

Go to our website—G2H-TMC.com—and listen to our artists. Request them on your local radio stations, because you know the conglomerates will never play our songs unless you force them to.

Buy our music—at G2H-TMC.com or wherever CDs are sold. We know you'll want to buy the music, instead of download, because the money goes to the artists.

You also write a second concept based on the idea we read about in the literature—the one about the labels making their own Napster. Again, this is to present a couple of different concepts to consumers. Who knows, they might like the one from the literature better than yours. But, based on your working theories, you don't think that will be the case.

The second concept is:

"LABELS FOR YOU"—BETTER THAN NAPSTER—FOR ONLY $9.99 A MONTH

Now you can access and download from a huge selection of music offered by all the major labels.

All the major labels—Sony, BMG, Universal, Warner, etc.—have banded together to offer you their music catalogs on the Internet.

For $9.99 a month you can access this huge catalog and download and own up to fifteen songs per month.

Besides huge selection, you get the highest-quality digital sound possible (much better than what is available on file-sharing sites) and a guarantee that everything you download will be virus free.

Plus, as a subscriber you get special deals on label merchandise.

STEP #4: FINANCIAL DUE DILIGENCE

You have an idea. Maybe consumers will like it and maybe they won't. But if they do, will it make Bill lots of money? An idea, however popular it is with consumers, is not any good unless it drives substantial revenue.

Before you go ask people if the idea is any good, you need to do some back-of-the-envelope projections. If those come out marginal, you need to go back to the drawing board on come up with other ideas.

Curiously, most really good ideas don't require extensive analysis to make a first cut at whether they are worth a lot of money.

Our experience is the smaller the idea, the more analysis required to "prove" the idea out. In fact, when it comes to developing big ideas, beware if the financial analysis is burdening.

Big ideas that reinvent businesses are not "rounding errors" on a spreadsheet—they usually feel more like a wild alligator with its nose in a noose and struggling to get free.

Back to our music example. You have to spend some time at this stage to be pretty sure your projections are right. In the case of our new music co-op, it is making assumptions about how many consumers will like the idea and how many CDs those consumers will buy from the co-op (instead of downloading for free), determining revenue based on the number of CDs we think they will buy and subtracting costs (product costs, artist co-op payments, etc.). Bill gets what is left. After doing some back-of-envelope math, the numbers say that if we are even close with our assumptions, this is a business worth pursuing. Remember the purpose of this step is not to get highly accurate estimates of consumer demand and revenue, but to make sure you have an idea that—with reasonable assumptions—makes sense financially. It is amazing how many ideas don't make the grade at this point. So this becomes another place to catch bad ideas before they get further downstream.

STEP #5: TALK TO CONSUMERS ONE AT A TIME

We've done our learning, we have developed our working theories, we have developed ideas and written concepts from those working theories, and we have done some basic financial due diligence. Now it is time to see what we have from the only perspective that matters—that of the consumer.

We talk to consumers one-on-one, one at a time. It is critical to speak to consumers in this manner.

> You have to put in the time listening to consumers one at a time if you want to develop successful ideas. Period.

In talking to people one-on-one, you invite representatives of the target market (music listeners who buy and/or download music) to a research facility where you present the concepts and get their reaction.

The interviews are typically an hour long. You want to interview a decent number of people so you can be reasonably sure whether or not your ideas have potential. You can often get a good idea by interviewing about thirty representative consumers. But if your working theories and concepts are wrong, you may have to start all over, which could mean another thirty consumers. Interviewing and listening to consumers will take a lot of time (30 interviews x 1 hour each = 30 hours). But if you want to be successful, you have to do it. This is a time-consuming process, but in the end it is far less time consuming than working on basketfuls of new product ideas that meet their doom in the marketplace.

In this case, here is an exercise you would probably want to do with consumers when you sit down with them:

On this sheet is a description of a new music service that may be introduced in the future, depending upon what consumers think about the idea. Please take a moment to read this and then we'll talk about it.

The Good Guys' Honest, Trueblue Music Co-op (G2H-TMC)

At G2H-TMC, it's not about money, it's about music.

A collaborative music cooperative, owned by the artists, not the conglomerates.

Created to bring great, distinctive music to you, the music lover.

Created to give the artists, finally, what they are worth and deserve.

Created to give you music for a value. We've taken the middleman conglomerates out of the equation that means we can sell the music for a lot less—and the money goes to the artists, not the conglomerates.

Go to our website—G2H-TMC.com—and listen to our artists. Request them on your local radio stations, because you know the conglomerates will never play our songs unless you force them to.

Buy our music—at G2H-TMC.com or wherever CDs are sold. We know you'll want to buy the music, instead of download, because the money goes to the artists.

Then you ask questions like these:

What are your thoughts and feelings about this idea?

What, if anything, do you like about it?

What, if anything, do you dislike about it?

Would you be more likely to buy music from this service than from record labels?

You currently download most of the music you listen to for free. And you only bought one CD in the last twelve months. Let's say this service came out with ten CDs in the next year that you liked. *How many of those would you download for free and how many would you buy?*

And we would ask similar questions about the other concept, as follows:

On this sheet is a description of another new music service that may be introduced in the future, depending upon what consumers think about the idea. Please take a moment to read this and then we'll talk about it.

"Labels For You"—Better Than Napster—For Only $9.99 a Month

Now you can access and download from a huge selection of music offered by all the major labels.

All the major labels—Sony, BMG, Universal, Warner, etc.—have banded together to offer you their music catalogs on the Internet.

For $9.99 a month you can access this huge catalog and download up to fifteen songs per month.

Besides a huge selection, you get the highest-quality digital sound possible (much better than what is available on file-sharing sites) and a guarantee that everything you download will be virus free.

Plus, as a subscriber you get special deals on label merchandise.

Again, you would ask questions like these...

What are your thoughts and feelings about this idea?

What, if anything, do you like about it?

What, if anything, do you dislike about it?

Would you be more likely to buy music from this service than from the individual record labels?

You currently download most of the music you listen to for free. And you only bought one CD in the last twelve months. Let's say this service came out with ten CDs in the next year that you liked. *How many of those would you download for free and how many would you buy?*

At this point you have learned a lot about what consumers like and dislike about your ideas for a new record label, because you have spent many hours listening to them. The next step is done more or less at the same time you interview consumers. Simply put, as you begin to hear what folks like and dislike, you use what you hear to modify and improve the idea.

STEP #6: ITERATE THE CONCEPTS BY LISTENING TO CONSUMERS

No concept or idea, as originally written, is perfect. So you have to modify it as you listen to consumers.

In this case, you did a really good job. Most consumers really liked the first idea. But they need a little more information:

- They want to know how much of the money actually goes to the artists.
- They want to know, specifically, how much the co-op will be selling CDs for.

Given that feedback, you rewrite the concept:

The Good Guys' Honest, Trueblue Music Co-op (G2H-TMC)

At G2H-TMC, it's not about money, it's about music.

A collaborative music cooperative, owned by the artists, not the conglomerates.

Created to bring great, distinctive music to you, the music lover.

Created to give the artists, finally, what they are worth and deserve—*70 percent of profits go to the artists*—*only 30 percent goes to administration of the co-op.*

Created to give you music for a value. We've taken the middleman conglomerates out of the equation which means we can sell the music for a lot less—*most of our CDs sell for $6 to $9*—and the money goes to the artists, not the conglomerates.

Go to our website—G2H-TMC.com—and listen to our artists. Request them on your local radio stations, because you know the conglomerates will never play our songs unless you force them to.

Buy our music—at G2H-TMC.com or wherever CDs are sold. We know you'll want to buy the music, instead of download, because the money goes to the artists.

As it turns out, many of the people in the interviews love the co-op idea.

• They like the fact that the co-op is not a conglomerate.
• They like the fact the artists get most of the money.
• They like the $6 to $9 price point.

Your working theories, as demonstrated in the idea, prove out. There is an opportunity to be the good guy in an industry that the public perceives to be filled with villains.

By the way, you also found out that the idea from the literature—a Napster created by the labels—is bad news. And once again your working theories prove out. Consumers were not going to buy from the individual labels because they see them as bad guys. They were certainly not going to buy from them when they banded together. This was perceived as even worse than the current situation—a conglomeration of conglomerates trying to take even more money.

Scrap that idea. Some consumers might pay $10 a month to an organization they like and respect, but few to none are going to do so to the villain—even though the villain might offer some huge selection, quality, and security.

STEP #7: TAKE THE BEST CONCEPTS COMING OUT OF THE INTERVIEWS AND MONETIZE THEM: PREDICT REAL-WORLD REVENUE

Time to find out how big that opportunity is.

So you take the best concept, and monetize it—that is, predict its real-world revenue. You do that by:

1. Doing a large scale survey—eight hundred to one thousand quantitative interviews with target consumers.
2. In the survey, you ask questions similar to the ones asked in the interviews.
3. You model the data back from the survey to project revenue.

The survey is done over the telephone or on the Internet. This is a step where you want the guidance of market research pros that know how to turn survey data into reliable, real-world estimates. We like seasoned gray hair (or no hair) pros for this part because it is technically complex.

The core questions you ask consumers look like this:

Let's say this service came out with ten CDs in the next year that you liked.

How many of the ten CDs would you purchase from this new service?

When you get the survey data back, you model the revenue. The model shows that this idea is going to make Bill (remember Bill, the billionaire?) a lot of money.

You call up Bill and say, "Bill, this is Andy. I've got your answer. You're going to be involved in the music business as the good guy, the hero, which should be a lot of fun. Plus you are going to make a lot of money—projections are on the way to you. Plus, a lot of other people are going to be happy too—music fans, for instance, and artists. It's win-win-win."

And Bill says, "Great, Andy, I knew you would come up with a solution. You have the seven-step system."

And you say, "Well, talk to you later, Bill, got to go." Because you've got to get on another project. The eighth richest person in the world called you yesterday, and he needs you to find him a way to make lots of money in the cable television business (yes, the cable television business that is, at the moment, a complete mess). He's looking to have some fun and he wants to move up from the eighth spot.

CHAPTER 13

BEDROCK: IT'S MORE THAN FRED AND WILMA'S HOMETOWN

One of the cornerstones of Idea Engineering system, and the lightning in a bottle that it creates, is "going to bedrock."

Bedrock is not just the town where Fred and Wilma Flintstone live.

> Bedrock is the foundation for what consumers think and do—why they buy certain products, why they buy those products at certain stores, what they truly, really think of new products, and what makes them tick.

If you are going to come up with ideas that drive large revenue gains, you have to go to bedrock.

Oddly, new-product and idea-development efforts are almost never designed to get to bedrock. In focus groups, for instance, with eight to ten consumers participating, the moderator does not have time to drill deep and find out the real why. A focus group lasts two hours—120 minutes. Fifteen minutes is spent at the front explaining how the group works and having everybody introduce themselves. That leaves 105 minutes, if you start on time. Say the group is supposed to discuss six major topics (and many groups deal with more than that), it works out to a little over two minutes per person per topic.

> At two minutes per person per topic, you cannot dive deep. You can only skate on the surface...and the surface is almost always misleading or wrong.

With two minutes per person per topic, the market research people running the show are often more concerned with just getting through the material rather than getting the right answer. The moderator must try to achieve consensus on a topic as quickly as possible—there is no time to deal with the shades of gray.

Participants whose opinions do not seem to make sense are discounted, as there just isn't enough time to ask follow-up questions (viewers in the back room often make fun of these participants—something that is done at their own peril, since these are customers and potential customers).

Votes are often taken in focus groups to speed the process along. In trying to determine whether people like bleu cheese with hot wings, the moderator asks: "Who likes bleu cheese? Let's see a show of hands." Two people raise their hands fully, three more raise their hands about halfway, and another respondent lifts a finger. "Okay," the moderator says, "that's six who like bleu cheese and only two who don't." Conclusion: almost everybody likes bleu cheese....

...except that the three who had their hands up halfway like bleu cheese on salads, but would never dip chicken wings in bleu cheese, and the person who raised a finger only the likes his mother's homemade bleu cheese dressing (he would never try bleu cheese dressing in a restaurant). So almost everybody does *not* like bleu cheese on chicken wings—the opposite of what the moderator concluded.

When you just skim the surface by racing through material, you are skating, skimming the surface, accepting the quick, easy (but often wrong) answer. Skating does not help your career or produce big revenue gains. Eventually it gets you fired. In the meantime, it wastes a lot of the company's time and money.

> To come up with big ideas that drive big revenue gains, *you have to go to bedrock*.

SO...HOW DO YOU GET TO BEDROCK?

Like everything else in this book, it can be learned, and bad habits can be pushed away. To get to bedrock, you have to:

- Put in the time
- Be patient
- Listen
- Trust the people you are listening to
- Dig until you know what the consumer means

Put in the Time

You already know what that means. It means talking to people one at a time for forty-five minutes to an hour. Talk to thirty people, which adds up to thirty hours.

Be Patient

Interviewing people one at a time is not usually entertaining. Individual, in-depth interviews are a hike from the first interview to the last one, one step down the trail, another one, keeping a steady pace so you don't burn out.

If your working theories are good and your resulting concepts and ideas are good, everything will work out in the end, if you just keep taking the steps.

- Don't make the mistake of jumping to conclusions after a couple of interviews.
- Don't think you have it figured out early.
- Be patient and listen to each consumer who comes through. It will all fit together by the end.

Listen

We are talking about intense listening, where you do nothing except listen. Often, we don't listen or we half listen. Maybe human beings in general have lost their ability to really listen intently, or maybe they never had it, but this is certainly the case for people observing consumer interviews from behind a one-way mirror.

> Everyone likes to talk, but no one wants to listen.

Not listening during consumer interviews falls into two categories. One is now that we have escaped the office, it is time to make telephone calls, send emails, catch up on what has been happening with the company, gossip, and generally do anything and everything but listen to what the consumer is saying. This is not the kind of intense listening that you need in order to understand what consumers want.

The second category is more dangerous than the first. It is listening, but listening *judgmentally,* which is worse than not listening at all.

Here is how it works. We are conducting one-on-one interviews and marketing people are observing from behind a one-way mirror. A respondent comes into the interviewing room. The interviewer starts talking to the respondent.

Somebody in the back room dislikes the respondent—he or she is dressed funny or looks different (lip ring, dyed red hair) or does not speak in an articulate manner or says something that, on the surface, does not make sense. And so people in the back room make fun of the respondents and discount anything and everything they say.

LISTENING JUDGMENTALLY IS VERY BAD

You must not listen judgmentally or you risk missing the real message. Not all your customers dress well or speak well or say things the way you say them. But they are your customers (or your potential customers), and to sweep their opinions away because they are different from who you talk to in meetings and see in the hallway at work is to court absolute disaster.

Here's an example. We were conducting an Idea Engineering project for Blockbuster Video. The topic was how Blockbuster can compete more effectively selling DVDs. Blockbuster sells some DVDs, but the lion's share of the market belongs to the discounters (Wal-Mart, etc.).

So this kid, maybe eighteen years old, comes into the interviewing room. The interviewer talks to him a bit, and it is apparent the kid is not particularly articulate, at least in terms of the "MBA talk" the interviewer and the back room people use. Before things get far along, some of the people in the back room are saying this is going to be a waste of an interview.

The interviewer shows the kid the concept—it is an idea about how Blockbuster can *sell* DVDs in the store. The kid reads the concept through. The interviewer asks the kid what he thinks about the concept. The kid thinks for a while and says:

"I rent movies at Blockbuster."

Not particularly insightful. At least that is what the interviewer and the people in the back room observing are thinking. So the interviewer, thinking the kid did not understand the concept, reads it to him. Then he asks, again, what the kid thinks about the idea. And the kid repeats again, "I rent movies at Blockbuster." Hmm. Can't get him off that dime. He must not understand the question yet.

The interviewer says, "Right, but Blockbuster says here they are going to start selling movies at Blockbuster, and the price is pretty good, and they are going to have a pretty good selection and you're in there renting movies anyway a couple of times a week, so it would be more convenient for you to buy movies at Blockbuster. That's what they are saying in this...so what do you think of they idea?"

The kid says, "I *rent* movies at Blockbuster. I *buy* movies at Wal-Mart." This is an improvement, but not much of one in the mind of the interviewer and the people in the back room. What everyone wants the kid to talk about are the features in the concept—the price of the movies, the selection, the convenience. What is his reaction to those, how can they be improved, what should be added or subtracted? But the kid can't get past square one.

The interviewer—frustrated—reads through the concept again and says, "I don't think you understand what they are saying here.

And the kid, after thinking a moment says, "Yeah, I understand. You're the one doesn't get it. It doesn't matter what you say, Blockbuster is where you *rent* movies."

Only one guy in the back room is really listening—listening nonjudgmentally—and he understands exactly what the kid is saying. It is not that the kid is dumb or can't think logically or doesn't get it. He gets it plenty. He gets it crystal clear.

It's us who don't get it. The kid is saying it doesn't matter which specific features we offer to entice him to buy DVDs at Blockbuster. None of that matters to him. After being told for his entire lifetime that Blockbuster is a place to rent, it is hard for him to think of Blockbuster as a place to buy. He is saying Blockbuster has done its job well—he thinks of the store as *the* movie rental place. It is much harder for him to envision Blockbuster as a place that also sells movies.

This eighteen-year-old has identified a significant issue—how to transition the consumer perception of Blockbuster from rental to rental *and* sales. And he has said that the concept we showed him does not do this, that our idea needs more work to make it sizzle. Finally everyone listened. Blockbuster has been masterful at reinvention over the years, and the idea goes back to the drawing board for more work—until it sizzles.

> *Only* if you listen nonjudgmentally—only if you take the time and are patient—do you understand what the kid is saying.
> Otherwise you miss the core issue.
> You miss everything.

The most successful people often have one thing in common—an inordinate ability to listen (even if they, themselves, like to talk a lot).

H. Wayne Huizenga, the only person in U.S. business history to start three *Fortune* companies from scratch, is this way. You would present to him or sit in meetings with him and he would simply listen, always alert, always intent, always watching.

He has eyes that drilled right through you. What he was doing was going to bedrock, taking the time, being patient, not jumping to conclusions. Listening, waiting for it to come together. And his success though the years shows how that technique works.

Listening well is a learned skill. It is not magic but it does take concentration and focus. Turn off the BlackBerrys and cell phones, and give your full and undivided attention to the person sitting in front of you who is being interviewed.

In our practice, we always use two people to listen. It works like this: we have the person interviewed for forty-five minutes or an hour, and two of us listening and making notes. It may sound like overkill but it is not. We'd recommend you do the same thing—have two people listening as consumers talk about your ideas. You will be amazed at the subtle and useful details this technique reveals.

Part of listening is also watching body language, like looking for the folded hands ("I'm not interested" or "I've already decided"), or leaning into the conversation ("Tell me more"), and so on.

Listening is a skill that improves with practice, and Idea Engineering gives you plenty of opportunity to practice.

Trust the People You Are Listening To

This is similar to listening nonjudgmentally. When a consumer steps into the interviewing room and starts to talk, you have to have a basic faith or trust that what they are saying is what they believe.

This idea runs counter to the attitude you sometimes see—distrust or discounting of consumer opinions given in a research setting. Some of this distrust may come from the fact that companies have been burned so often by focus groups. But we are not talking about focus groups here. We are talking about interviewing people one at a time. In focus groups, there is a lot of interaction, political correctness, and strong-willed people affecting the opinions of weak-willed people and participants who do not appear to have an opinion.

In one-on-one interviews, there is, for the interviewee, no place to hide. There is much less pressure to express politically correct opinions. There are no other participants with whose opinions he/she can agree with before considering their own.

Another problem is making excuses when we don't like what we hear. Any kind of qualitative research with consumers—where you are talking to small numbers of people—can be criticized:

- The people that are being interviewed are being paid, so they are probably just making it up.
- The market research company recruits people from their database—they are professional respondents.
- They don't look or talk like our customers.

Put all these and any other excuses for not listening out of your mind when the respondent walks in. Show some basic trust. If there is a problem with a respondent, the interviewer will detect that and deal with it. But in the vast majority of cases, the person who comes in is just a consumer who will speak his/her mind in the one-on-one setting and to whom you need to listen.

> Ninety-nine percent of consumers know why they buy various products and why they buy them at specific stores.

Their reasons almost always make sense and have internal logic if you listen nonjudgmentally long enough and have a basic sense of trust in what they say.

Listen, be patient, listen nonjudgmentally, and trust.

Dig in Until You Know What the Consumers Means

When you talk to consumers for an hour about one subject, you have plenty of time to really find out what they think. So do it! This is the time where your success depends on finding out what truly motivates the person you are speaking to. Make sure you dig until you find out.

- Do not be satisfied with the superficial.
- Make sure you probe until you have a very clear idea in your head—something so clear you could explain it on a Post-It note to the office intern—as to why someone does what they do or feels the way they do.

Although consumers know why they do things, their why is not always on the surface of their brains. They do not think about why and where they buy things nearly as much as we do. In fact, they hardly think about these things at all. So, if you ask a consumer why they bought a DVD at Wal-Mart, their first response is probably not the sole explanation. Consumers usually have a number of reasons for doing certain things. You have to dig for the other reasons.

Additionally, they will often rationalize their actions and beliefs. Human behaviors are more often based on emotions than they are logic and a studious weighing of pros and cons. But everybody talks about their behavior in logical, rational terms. You have to dig to get to the emotional base.

There are a variety of interviewing techniques designed to get below the surface. Some interviewers use projective techniques—role-playing or using visual stimuli, free expression, or thematic apperception tests.

> We prefer a more direct approach known as laddering. Basically, it consists of asking the consumer why— badgering them in a gentle way, if necessary—until they themselves fully understand the motivations for their behavior and can explain it to the interviewer.

In almost all cases, consumers can self-analyze why they do certain things with "why" probing and with the interviewer pointing out apparent contradictions in what the consumer is saying (and there are often contradictions).

Whatever technique you use or have your interviewer use, make sure, again, that you understand fully each consumer who is interviewed. Don't skate. Don't skim the surface. Dig in until you truly understand.

There is nothing magic about the process for developing new products and services that work. But the closest thing to magic may be the chapter just covered: the art and science listening, of getting the unvarnished truth about what consumers think. The recommendations in this chapter are meant to be taken very literally. Follow the specific suggestions given. Folks that have taken this advice report an immediate and dramatic improvement in understanding their customers' needs, wishes, and desires.

CHAPTER 14

WHAT INTERVIEWS WITH THOUSANDS OF CONSUMERS TAUGHT US

We have interviewed thousands of people—one at a time. Talking to thousands of people, one at a time, you learn something about people—about how they think, why they buy, why they don't, what they like, what they hate.

Here are a few things we have learned about consumers in the new millennium—who they are and how they think. These are some of the finer details that will help you boost your new product success rate and supercharge your Idea Engineering efforts.

1. Consumers are smart.
2. Keep it simple.
3. Girls just want to have fun—boys too.
4. They don't care how much it costs.
5. They're bored.
6. They are all different.

Let's look at each of these findings.

CONSUMERS ARE SMART

There are a couple of famous quotes that illustrate an attitude that some companies have toward consumers.

There is a sucker born every minute.

—David Hannum (not P. T. Barnum)

No one in this world, so far as I know—and I have researched the records for years, and employed agents to help me—has ever lost money by underestimating the intelligence of the great masses of the plain people. Nor has anyone ever lost public office thereby.

—H. L. Mencken

This attitude will not get you far in America's competitive market for goods and services. Consumers are smart. They know what they want. They know what they don't want.

It is amazing to listen to people in our interviews who, you are pretty sure, would score in the bottom 1 percent on any standardized test. These are people who do not know the meaning of simple words or phrases, people who have trouble expressing even the smallest thoughts. But they know whether your idea is any good or not.

> ## They know, within seconds of you describing it, if they will buy what you want to sell them.

As a matter of fact, we would say the exact opposite of the two quotes listed above. There may be a sucker born every minute, but few of them are consumers. Most of them are businesses thinking they can sell things that make little or no sense to consumers. And, in fact, many businesses have lost tons of money underestimating the intelligence of plain people.

Consumers, the basic folks out there, are smart when it comes to buying stuff. They know what they want and what they do not want. You might fool them into buying something once. But if the product does not deliver on what you told them, they will never buy it again—and they will not be happy with you for fooling them the first time.

What consumers want is simple: they want things that satisfy their needs and solve their problems. And they know what their needs and problems are without really having to think about them.

Businesses run into trouble (become "suckers born every minute") because they forget (or never learn) that products and services always have to be consumer based—that is, they have to satisfy needs and solve problems.

If we know one thing, it is this—to develop great ideas, you have to have a lot of respect for the wisdom of plain people.

KEEP IT SIMPLE

Consumers—the basic folks out there—are smart. That does not mean they want to spend a lot of time trying to figure out what you are trying to sell them.

YOU HAVE TO KEEP IT SIMPLE.

It is not that they are unable to figure out complex offers. They could if they wanted to. They don't want to. They do not consider it their job—they consider it your job.

You are off track:

- If they have to think about your basic proposition for longer than three seconds
- If the offer in any way does not make sense or leaves important questions unanswered
- If what you say contains a single word, the meaning of which they are unsure—or a single word they do not like

They are gone, not to be back. It's because you have not done your job. They move on to other offers.

The average person gets propositioned a thousand times a day between television, radio, in-store signage, billboards, online advertising, and direct mail.

There is no need for them to expend mental energy on your offer. They know that within the next several seconds, another will be speeding at them. If the next offer is simple and clear, and satisfies one of their needs or solves one of their problems, they just might take it. But your offer is already back there, in the past, behind. It had its chance, its brief second in the sun, and the people have moved on without you.

You can have a product that satisfies an important need or solves a critical problem, but if the product is described in too complex a manner, you are lost.

One of the hardest things is making something simple. It is hard to make simple things simple, much less complex things. Some great products—products that satisfy a need and should sell like hotcakes—can never be described in simple enough terms to get them into mass market.

TiVo, using technology referred to as digital video recording, is a great example. TiVo is a product that everyone who buys loves. *It changed my life. Now I love to watch TV.* But TiVo has never found a way to simply express what its product does in a way that resonates with consumers. And so it has had trouble getting into homes. Make no mistake—it is revolutionary, and is probably the future of television. But its acceptance is slowed by the difficulty in simply explaining what it does.

If we know two things, one is that consumers are smart. The second one is that you have to express your core benefit very, very simply—so simply that it takes three seconds or less to get.

GIRLS JUST WANT TO HAVE FUN—BOYS, TOO!

Life can be, well, not fun. You don't know if you'll have your job tomorrow. Your 401K, which two years ago was almost to the point you could retire, is now dragging bottom. Your best friend's wife, without warning, woke up and said she wants a divorce. You're wondering if your wife (or husband) might do the same. And then there is war, pestilence, and famine.

There are so many bad things than can and do happen, people want to have fun whenever they can. They want to be entertained, they want to escape. As long as the world is crazy and bad things happen, entertainment will be a great business to be in.

The amount of time consumers devote to entertainment goes up every year. The amount of time they spend watching movies and television, listening to music, etc. increases every year, presumably at the expense of things that are not fun.

So consumers clearly want to have fun. But American business is not very often set up for fun. We believe that:

- Fun is an immensely powerful competitive weapon that can drive revenue.
- Fun is vastly underused by American business.
- Consumers will pay more and seek out places, products, and services that offer fun over competitors that do not.

The end-goal of many consumer businesses may be something different from today. The end-goal may be not customer satisfaction ("How satisfied are you—very satisfied, somewhat satisfied…"), but "smiles."

> **Walt Disney once hired George Gallup to measure the number of people smiling as they left Disneyland. Disneyland is still doing okay.**

A foolproof roadmap to making business fun and entertaining does not exist. Many retailtainment/shoppertainment ventures (Warner Brothers stores, Nickelodeon stores, Coca-Cola stores, Viacom stores, Planet Hollywood, Rainforest Café) have failed.

But we have sat across from enough consumers to know that fun has star power. Read a simple idea like the following:

WHO'S GOT THE BEST EXCUSE?
A new game at Blockbuster Video. Write down your best excuse for being late with your movies. Drop it in the fish bowl. Each week, Blockbuster will pick the best excuses. The winners will get a "Get Out of Jail" card, good for the extended viewing fees the next time you bring your movies back late.

People laugh and smile. *Laugh and smile!* Because this is something different. A fun thing stands out because American business is most often not about fun.

There are few experts on fun and using fun in American business. Talking to consumers about fun and analyzing the failures, we have learned a couple of things. One, if you want to establish fun, you need a culture that lives fun from top to bottom. For a company to be successful with fun, it needs fun at the top.

Another thing we have learned is that companies should not sink lots of money into hard-asset based fun. Retailtainment has failed largely because companies made heavy capital outlays—Rainforest Café, for instance. Large capital outlay means that the offering cannot be changed easily or often. But consumers bore quickly. They need to constantly see the offering refreshed.

And, finally, we have learned that:

Consumers will pay for fun.

Give them the choice between a fun product or service and one that does the job but does not provide fun extras, they always pick the fun one. Fun means picking up market share.

THEY DON'T CARE HOW MUCH IT COSTS
Warning: This Section Applies Only to Entertainment. All Other Industries Beware.

When it comes to entertainment, within reason, people do not care how much it costs. If you give them exactly what they want, they will gladly pay.

This flies in the face of conventional wisdom. When the cable company raises its rates, there is a public outcry. When the theater chain raises ticket prices by fifty cents, a movie goer says, "I'm going to be spending my entertainment dollar elsewhere." Commonly, people who rent movies say the prices are way too high. And on it goes.

But these are the facts:

- Cable and satellite penetration is at an all-time high—88 percent of television households have one or the other.
- People drop cable more often to switch to more expensive satellite packages than they do to "get back" at the cable company for raising prices.
- The switch from cable to satellite has, in most cases, been fueled by a desire for more programming (satellite has, historically, carried more channels) rather than a desire to cut entertainment costs.
- People will pay more to get what they want.

Another example is that movie rentals from video stores were down in the last few years, but total spending for movies at home just keeps going up, up, up. To the tune of over $20 billion dollars a year.

- The reason movie rentals were down is that DVD sales were up. In other words, people were increasingly buying instead of renting.
- A rental costs around $4. A DVD costs $10 to $24 to buy. So that is not what you would call a savings.
- People will pay to get what they want.

Over and over, we see this phenomenon when we sit down and talk to people. They complain that entertainment is too expensive—they threaten to drop their cable, rent fewer movies, and go to the movies less if prices are raised.

> But when it comes to it, they really do not care how much it costs.

This needs to be within reason, of course. They will not pay $14 to go to a movie when the rate at most theaters is $6 to $9. But they will pay $8 instead of $6 if one theater has stadium seating and the other does not. And they will pay $4.00 for a movie rental if that store has a much better selection than a store that charges $3.00. And they will pay $60 to get the channels they want with the satellite company even though the cable company charges $45, but does not have all those channels.

Another important point is that although consumers talk about how expensive entertainment is, many (or most) do not really know what the prices are, or what they really spend on entertainment. Say a movie rental store charges $4 to rent a movie. Ask a sampling of its customers how much it costs to rent a movie, about a third will say $3, about a third will say $5, and the rest of the people will be all over the board. Less than a quarter of folks will actually know it is $4.

- **Entertainment is about fun.**
- **Anything that gets in the way of fun is bad.**
- **Thinking about what things costs is not fun.**

They same applies to cable and satellite bills. Few know how much their television costs. Someone whose cable costs $50 a month is more likely to say $65 or $40 than $50.

> In entertainment, people will pay for value.
> Value does not necessarily mean the lowest price.
> In fact, when it comes to entertainment, higher
> prices often equal higher value. Especially when you
> include "more stuff I want."

THEY'RE BORED

We mentioned the "hedonic treadmill" in a previous chapter, which means:

People adapt to improving circumstances to the point of affective neutrality. An experience that is routine and fully expected becomes affectively neutral.

This is an actual psychological principal, studied, documented, and tested with rodents. It is a fancy way of saying people get bored quickly. We are not all that different from rodents—at least in some ways.

And people do get bored quickly. As we said earlier, the main reason many of the retailtainment ventures failed is due to the hedonic treadmill. People waited in line to get into the Rainforest Café. They finally got a seat and marveled at the animal robots and the jungle sounds—it was just like a rain forest. The food was okay, but, boy oh boy, what about the atmosphere!

A few months later they went again. The Rainforest, the second time around, was interesting, but not as spectacular as the first time, because nothing had changed. Already, after only two visits, it is getting old. The food was okay, and it sure wasn't cheap. The hedonic treadmill takes another one down.

> The speed with which the consumer becomes bored is something you should always keep in mind.

It does not matter how good your new product is when it is introduced. Before it is introduced, you have to be thinking about how you are going to improve it. You have to constantly refresh and redefine your offering.

THEY ARE ALL DIFFERENT

Interviewing people one at a time, you come to appreciate that each person is unique. That is one of the great side-benefits of one-on-one interviews—you have the opportunity to see and enjoy humanity in some of its many, distinct imprints. It is an ongoing movie. Here are a few examples.

Sitting in an interviewing room—just a conference room with a one-way mirror—is a male, age twenty-four. We are talking about various aspects of fast-food restaurants. Where do you go? What do you order? What do you like about it?

He is a good-looking kid, nicely dressed, works in an entry-level job in the insurance business, well-spoken, a college graduate, single, lives alone, and eats out three to five times a week.

We get to talking about a new menu item. We describe it and get his feedback. He likes it. We say, "What if this costs $3.60?"

He says, "That's fine, except make it $4.00."

And the interviewer says, "Excuse me?"

And he says, "Make it $4.00."

The interviewer says, "I'm sorry. I don't understand. Why would you want to pay forty cents more than I quoted you? Are you saying it's worth forty cents more?"

He says, "I don't like change," meaning coins.

This is something we have not heard before.

He goes on, "See, everything would be so much faster if you didn't have to deal with change. Think about it. How much of your time is taken up with digging in your pants to find the correct change? How much of your time is wasted waiting for counter clerks giving you change?"

The interviewer does not know and cannot respond.

"Quite a lot," he says. "My idea is that everything should be an even dollar amount. Just round up or down to the nearest dollar. If you are charging $5.35 now, round down to $5.00. If you are charging $5.55, round up to $6.00. Everybody's life will be easier."

Here is a person who, we have determined from previous questions, spends Sundays during the football season parked on the couch watching games from morning into the night and averages thirty-four hours of television a week.

His idea of saving time is rounding prices up or down so he does not have to wait for change. Assuming an average of three commercial transactions a day, seven days a week, fifty-two weeks a year, doing away with change would save him ninety-one minutes a year, 4 percent of the time he spends watching TV in the average *week*.

Here is another example of how each human is unique. Sitting in an interviewing room is a female, age fifty-six, married, three kids, but they are all gone, works in a bank. We are talking about movies.

The interviewer asks, "How many times do you go to the theater to see movies in the average month?"

The woman says, "Sixteen."

The interviewer says, "Sixteen, wow that is a lot; four times a week. Now, with your cable, you have HBO, Cinemax, Showtime, Starz, The Movie Channel, Encore. Pretty much all the extra movie channel the cable company offers. How many movies do you watch on those channels in the average month?"

The woman says, "Eighty."

The interviewer says, "Geez, that's a lot of movies, something like 140 hours a month watching movies on the cable movie channels. Watching all those movies, you probably don't have much time to rent movies."

The woman says, "I rent about forty movies a month."

The interviewer adds it up—it comes to 136 movies a month. At a little over ninety minutes a movie, it adds up to almost sixty hours a week.

The woman says, "If I'm not working or in my car or sleeping, I'm watching movies."

Now that is a heavy user.

> Never forget that every human is unique. Some don't want to deal with pocket change. Others consume more of your product than you could ever imagine. They are all real, and they are all important. Get to know your customers so you know what they want in their products.

There is a fair amount to learn to get started with Idea Engineering, but the basics are pretty simple and you know them now. This chapter covered some of the finer points in conducting an Idea Engineering project. You can get a big head start in your own projects by knowing what we have learned about consumers and new products.

CHAPTER 15

DON'T WAIT FOR A MIRACLE

The nineties were a glorious time for businesspeople in America. It was the era of the dot-com, where possibilities were endless, and reality was only an occasional footnote. The nineties, some said, was all about putting a stake in the ground for doing business in the new millennium. It was a time to invest in new ideas, and in new ways of doing business. Wall Street and the venture capital community rewarded those who captured market share in their "space."

As the nineties and the dot-com explosion faded, some disappointed businesspeople just couldn't bear to watch the boom go bust. So they sought out a more traditional, old-fashioned way of making money—by lying, stealing, cheating, and cooking the books. The nineties are gone. The Internet has taken a rightful and important place in the world of commerce. Crooked businesspeople are getting caught, and we are back to the traditional business models where profit margins are expected, and price earnings ratios are back in fashion again.

Which brings us to today.

There has never been a better time than now to improve how you develop new products and services, to adopt a new way of thinking about how your company will reinvent itself with new products and services that your customers crave.

You don't need to wait for a miracle to happen in your new-product department. Here is a quick recap of how you can improve ideas, starting right now.

DECIDE IT IS TIME TO DO BETTER

Modern business is terribly inefficient at developing new products and services. We've settled in with a bag of tools that does not work well, which results in chasing ten or twenty ideas to find a single new product that is successful.

Big ideas are not random and unpredictable. They are not the product of paintball fights, deep meditation, exercises to generate one thousand ideas in two minutes, or navel gazing.

Like almost everything else—big ideas are the product of HARD WORK.

Most new products fail, but you have the power to change the odds in your favor. What has been lacking is a process—a proven method for developing ideas. Now there is a process that makes sense and that works. Use it, and you will get results. It is really that simple.

LOVE AFFAIRS HINDER BIG IDEA DEVELOPMENT

Many folks reading this book are executives, people that have the ability to direct how their companies pursue new products. A special word of advice for you captains, CEOs, COOs, CMOs, and others with this kind of authority:

> Avoid falling in love with your own ideas too quickly. Allow time for courtship, for romance, and for getting close.

Before you unleash all the love and passion for your own ideas, make sure your customers share your feelings (spurned lovers are a bad thing). Big ideas need a champion, and the bigger the idea, the greater the need for a big dog to move it through the organization.

CEOs and senior executives at big companies lead very different lives from most of us. What they like and what appeals to them is often very different. Life is different when you are in the top .5 percent in household income. So senior executives must be vigilant and take special care not to screen ideas solely through their own eyes.

What we are saying is this; don't fall in love with your own ideas until your consumers signal they are with you. Put *your* ideas into the seven-step process, too. If they spark, *then* you get behind and push.

ONLY BULL'S-EYES COUNT

Americans are overwhelmed with people trying to sell them something. Almost everything they hear gets tuned out.

Advertisers think they are delivering clearly crafted messages to consumers who are paying attention. Mostly, that is false. What consumers are hearing is blah, blah, blah, blah, blah—with an occasional word, or an occasional image that captures their attention. Everything else is getting screened out.

How do you rise above the clutter?

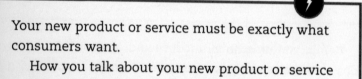

Your new product or service must be exactly what consumers want.

How you talk about your new product or service must be crisp, brief, and unambiguous.

Being just a few degrees off in your proposition, or the way you talk about your proposition, is the same as shooting in the opposite direction. In today's world of incredible choice and distribution for products and services, only bull's-eyes count.

How do you do shoot bull's-eyes? By putting discipline into your new-idea development. Listen to your consumers in an organized, proven way that lets you clearly hear what they want.

LESS IS MORE

The conventional thinking is that you need a lot of ideas to end up with one good idea, that you must generate a thousand ideas to come up with one winner. The truth is exactly the opposite. You need one or two great ideas at any given time—and everything else belongs in your idea trash pile. All the energy that goes into creating a list of a thousand ideas is wasted.

Your job is to identify those few ideas—the lightning in a bottle—that can make the tires burn for your company. Think "less" when it comes to the following aspects of idea development:

Less *ideas* should be pursued.

Less *people* should be involved in developing new products—especially in the early stages.

Less *words* should be used to describe and sell the new product when it is ready for the market.

The more things you are working on, the lower the odds that any one of them will succeed. The reason is diffusion of effort, and lack of focus.

Less *is* more.

RESIST THE URGE TO CARVE YOUR BUSINESS INTO NEEDY LITTLE BUCKETS

Think about it. Big companies get big mostly by finding a product that a lot of people will want to buy—and selling it to them. Computer-driven market segmentation tells you to do the opposite. It says that to be successful, you have to disassemble the thing that got you to the party—a mass-appeal proposition—and replace it with a half dozen or so small marketing segments, each of which needs its own marketing.

Unquestionably, there are cases where market segmentation makes sense. What you need to keep your radar screen up for are the artificial, computer-driven market segmentation schemes that have become fashionable over the past twenty years. And make no mistake—when you hear the words market segmentation today, it *almost always* refers to these artificial, computer-driven schemes. All too often, these end up in the circular file.

Focus instead on *aggregation*—how can I sell the most stuff to the largest number of people in the most efficient fashion?

Sound like common sense? Of course.

IF YOU DON'T SEEK, YOU WON'T FIND

The idea geniuses of our time—the Ted Turners, Sumner Redstones, Rupert Murdochs, and the like—are always looking for the next big idea. Their radar is always turned on. But idea moguls have a gift that most of us do not possess. Besides being constantly on the watch for ideas that can become big ideas, they have a talent for divining big ideas, separating the big ideas from everything else. Few of us have that talent.

The rest of us need training wheels, a process that helps narrow down a huge list of new product possibilities—to the one or two things that your company is going to do to make a big difference. When it comes to ideas for new products to reinvent and grow your business, your radar should always be turned on, too.

IF YOU WANT TO MAKE A BIG DIFFERENCE, START WITH SOMETHING BIG

Over and over again, large and sophisticated companies make the mistake of going after a much smaller audience than they should.

Here's a quick example. Let's say you are a successful manufacturer of high-quality men's shoes. You have national distribution through high-quality retailers, and your product line is mostly dress shoes. You capture a respectable 25 percent of men's dress shoe sales in America—far more than the number-two guy. Sales are flat and your marketing team suggests one of two alternatives:

- Introduce a full and complete line of summer sandals
- Introduce two new styles of men's dress shoes

You have never had a line of sandals before, and your distribution network has told you they will give you the display space. Adding a couple of new dress styles seems, well, boring.

What do you do? You dig in and start learning. You learn that only 18 percent of men own and wear sandals—hmmm. And that sandals only really sell about four months out of the year—another hmmm. By contrast, 85 percent of men own and wear dress shoes. And men's dress shoes sell year-round.

The problem with the sandals business is that right out of the gate your potential market has shrunk to less than one-fifth of the men in America. You have grossly limited your upside by starting with a small audience. You would want to weigh all the other variables and business situations, but all other things being equal, you need to go after big things if you want to make a big difference.

Going after a small audience makes life much harder than it needs to be. Why do they do it? Because companies don't believe they can come up with strong ideas that appeal to their mass customer base. They can. You can.

Harness the masses that already love you, and give them—all of them, if possible—new and better ways of doing business with you!

CREATE YOUR OWN LIGHTNING IN A BOTTLE!

So now we come to the end.

Are better ideas the key to better business results?

Are my company's skills in developing ideas on par with the skill we bring to other tasks?

Can you create lightning in a bottle?

You bet.

Decide to do it.

And do it.

You now know everything you need to get started.

ABOUT THE
AUTHORS

David Minter is one of the principals who lead Denver-based Minter + Reid, an idea-development group focused on bottom-line revenue generation for public and private companies in the areas of entertainment, media, retail, restaurant, food, and new technology.

Throughout his career, Minter has worked with high-growth companies to bring new ideas to the marketplace. Minter began his career at Motorola Inc., where he was responsible for product planning and competitive analysis. He then joined Dole Food Company, where he managed the analysis of international market information and was responsible for new business development.

Minter has spent much of his career working with Blockbuster, Inc. during the company's high-growth years. Minter was a senior marketing executive responsible for directing all consumer research, with specific expertise in entertainment, technology, and retail. Over the course of four years, he worked directly with H. Wayne Huizenga to open at least one store per day, increase market share, and unearth innovative consumer products and experiences for all business units, including Blockbuster Video, Blockbuster Music, Spelling Entertainment Corp., Republic Pictures, Blockbuster Park, Discovery Zone, Soundsational, the Florida Marlins, and the Florida Panthers. During the period that Blockbuster was majority owned by Viacom, Inc., Minter worked with other Viacom companies including Showtime Networks, MTV, and Nickelodeon.

Milestones include the introduction of videogames; expansion into the retail music business; investment into new entertainment ventures; and market introductions for DVD, video on demand, online rentals, and DirecTV pay-per-view. Minter was awarded Blockbuster's first patent. His work with Blockbuster, now in its second decade, has contributed to multibillion-dollar revenue growth and expansion from 500 stores to 8,500 stores.

In 1995, Minter relocated to Denver to help found Einstein-Noah Bagel Corporation, where he served as vice president of research and concept development. He was responsible for garnering consumer input for store design, product development, and brand management. Minter's contributions helped the company grow from zero to four hundred units in two years, and a successful IPO in 1996.

In addition to his role as principal of Minter + Reid, Minter is president of Minter & Associates, a marketing advisory and research consultancy he founded in 1997 that conducts high-level research work for clients throughout the U.S. and internationally. David also serves as VP-Marketing for Denver-based start-up company SmartCare Family

Medical Centers. Minter was recently awarded his second patent, which addresses commercializing Internet radio advertising. He earned his bachelor of business administration and master of business administration degrees, cum laude, from Florida Atlantic University, and lives with his wife and son near Denver, Colorado.

Michael Reid is one of two principals who lead Denver-based Minter + Reid. Reid's expertise includes design, management, and analysis of qualitative and quantitative research in telecommunications, entertainment, media, packaged goods, and utilities. He has helped several of the world's largest cable companies develop digital and telephony products; developed a new music-testing system for major labels to dramatically increase the odds that a new single will "chart"; and uncovered specific consumer preferences that helped the *New York Post* and *Denver Post* achieve the highest circulation growth in the newspaper industry.

Additionally, Reid has worked side-by-side with Minter in developing Blockbuster's online rental strategy, DVD in-store sales, and DVD trading—programs that contributed to Blockbuster's forty-seven-quarter record for continuous same-store sales growth.

Reid also is president of Paragon Media Strategies, a Denver-based full-service marketing and research company that generates actionable information for some of the world's largest media and entertainment companies, including News Corporation, Media News, Blockbuster, Susquehanna Communications, and Rogers Media. Paragon Media was founded in 1987, and employs more than seventy-five research and marketing professionals.

Reid earned his bachelor of arts at Doane College. As a Fulbright Scholar, he attended Phillips University (Marburg an der Lahn, Germany). He lives with his wife and children in Denver, Colorado.

INDEX